"Greg, if you tell me the truth, I will believe you. If you tell me a fact, I will listen. However, if you share with me a story, then I will remember."

—Lt. Roger Wildey, Special Operators Commander,

Santa Cruz County Sheriff's Office.

One of my first mentors on the path of the modern day warrior.

VICTORY!

SECOND EDITION

A PRACTICAL GUIDE TO
FORGING ~~ELITE~~ FITNESS
ETERNAL

VICTORY!
A PRACTICAL GUIDE TO FORGING ETERNAL FITNESS

SECOND EDITION

Copyright © 2019 Greg Amundson

ISBN 978-0-578-59765-2

ASIN XXX

By Greg Amundson

3703 Portola Drive, Santa Cruz, CA 95060

www.GregoryAmundson.com

Edited by Patti Bond

Layout and Design by Brooktown Design, www.brooktown.com

Illustrations by Joseph Carlos Fitzjarrell, www.fitznice.com

The author has done his best to articulate and illustrate God's Word by means of prayer, meditation and contemplation. Italics or brackets within a Scripture are the author's own emphasis.

Published by:
Eagle Rise Publishing, Virginia Beach, VA.
EagleRisePublishing.com

Printed and bound in the USA and UK on acid-free paper.
Additional books can be purchased through Amazon.

PRAISE FOR THE WORK OF GREG AMUNDSON

"I often tell people at my seminars, 'We don't need more Buddhists in the world, we need more Buddhas. We don't need more Christians, we need more Christ-like beings.' And such is the case with my amazing, breathing brother Greg Amundson. He's not one of those wishy-washy, praise the Lord, in-your-face, superficial Christians: He is a former SWAT Operator, DEA Special Agent, U.S. Army Captain, and CrossFit athlete and coach. He is a spiritual warrior, and he carries God in his heart. Greg's book *Victory* teaches the principles of spiritual development that can change your life."

—*Dan Brulé*, world renowned lecturer
and international bestselling author of *Just Breathe*

"Sometimes our mythic roots carry the most powerful insights, and Greg Amundson's fable, *The Warrior and The Monk*, is no exception. Greg leverages his remarkable storytelling ability to help the reader acquire new insights that serve to strengthen the spiritual core. Greg's new books, *Victory* and *Above All Else*, provide me with daily wisdom, revelation, and greater understanding of God's Word, in a way that only Greg can provide. It's a game changer."

—*Josh Mantz*, Former Army Major and
#1 Amazon bestselling author of *The Beauty of a Darker Soul*

"Greg fought the war on drugs, battled in the streets, on behalf of our nation. Now he fights to inspire us to overcome our fears, flaws, and failures, battling for the glory of God. Pick up, *Victory*, and *The Warrior and The Monk*, and let God's work, through Greg's words and stories, uplift your mind, body and soul."

—*Jay Dobyns*, *New York Times* bestselling author of
No Angel, and *Catching Hell*

"Greg's ability to transcend boundaries and speak to the essence of spirituality is profound and encouraging. By following the timeless advice in Greg's books, we can happily discover that what we are searching for has been within us the entire time."

—*Scott McEwen*, #1 *New York Times* bestselling co-author of
American Sniper; national bestselling *Sniper Elite* series,
and the new *Camp Valor* series of novels

"Greg Amundson's books, *Above All Else*, and *The Warrior and The Monk*, makes experiencing God a little more accessible. They are great primers for the new seeker and wonderful refreshment for the seasoned traveler."
—**Rev. Deborah L. Johnson**, Author of *The Sacred Yes* and *Your Deepest Intent*

"Greg Amundson's expert instruction has brought dramatically greater strength, balance, and vital energy into my daily life as it has the lives of countless others. Now, with *The Warrior and The Monk*, Greg guides us in channeling that newfound strength and energy toward a life of service, love, wisdom, and true fulfillment. A powerful and transformational book that will inspire you to live your very best life."
—**Girish**, musician, teacher, and author of *Music and Mantras: The Yoga of Mindful Singing for Health, Happiness, Peace and Prosperity*

"Greg Amundson's groundbreaking book, *The Warrior and The Monk*, is an inspiring, timely, and courageously articulated perspective on seeking (and discovering) a personal relationship with God. Greg's newest book, *Victory*, is a brilliant blueprint for integrating faith and fitness."
—**Robert Vera**, author of #1 Amazon bestseller, *A Warrior's Faith*, and founder of the Eagle Rise Speakers Bureau

"Greg's books, *Above All Else*, and *The Warrior and The Monk*, capture in words the epic quest we are all on to find happiness, meaning, and fulfillment in life. Greg articulates in a groundbreaking ministry that by turning our attention inward, and seeking God, we can find purpose in our life, and joy through being of service to others."
—**Karen Vaughn**, Gold Star mother of US Navy SEAL Aaron Carson Vaughn, and bestselling author of *World Changer: A Mother's Story*

"Greg Amundson is the epitome of a modern day warrior. He leads in all aspects of his life: As a warrior, as a Christian, and as a fitness expert. He writes with magical simplicity, yet is rigorous in his research and reasoning. As a leadership and motivation coach, when I need my own motivation I look to Greg Amundson. His track record of proving the validity of his message in his own life, and the lives that his message touches, is astounding. Greg's new book *Victory* is a vital tool for anyone interested in achieving the victory in their health, spirituality, fitness, and positive mental outlook on life."
—**Jason Redman**, Navy SEAL (ret.) and *New York Times* bestselling author of *The Trident: the Forging and Reforging of a Navy SEAL Leader*

"Greg is the epitome of the way we all should strive to be better each and every day. With grace, joy and a powerful passion to help others, he instills in all of us the beauty of life and the importance of following God. His books, *Above All Else*, and *The Warrior and The Monk*, will help you along your own path of self-discovery and reveal just how important you are in making this world a better place."

—**Kevin R. Briggs**, Sergeant, California Highway Patrol (Retired), and author of *Guardian of the Golden Gate, Protecting the Line Between Hope and Despair*

"Greg Amundson is a warrior with a monk-like mindset. His own self discovery and passion to help others is truly inspiring. Greg empowers us with the tools to a disciplined mind, spirituality, and perfect work-life balance."

—**Dr. Suhas Kshirsagar**, BAMS, MD(Ayu), author of #1 Amazon bestseller, *Change Your Schedule Change Your Life*

"Greg's new book *Victory* takes you inside the brilliant mind that has redefined the integration of Faith and fitness. Greg is one of the most prolific author's and speakers of our time, and his work will profoundly bless your life."

—**Dr. Gabrielle Lyon**, DO, Special Operations, Task Force Dagger

"The first step to self-mastery is reading Greg Amundson's work and considering the 'Way of the Warrior' as he is now teaching it."

—**Joe De Sena**, Spartan Founder & CEO and #1 *New York Times* bestselling author of *Spartan Up!*

"This book is a gift from Greg. His passion for integrating mind, body, and Spirit through his holistic training is inspiring, and can be a catalyst for you to do the same."

—**Mark Divine**, *New York Times* bestselling author of *The Way of the SEAL* and *Unbeatable Mind*

ALSO BY GREG AMUNDSON

Published Books

Your Wife is NOT Your Sister –
(And 15 other love lessons I learned the hard way)
Robertson Publishing – 2012

Firebreather Fitness –
Work Your Body, Mind and Spirit into the Best Shape of Your Life
(with TJ Murphy) Velo Press – 2016

The Warrior and The Monk –
A Fable About Fulfilling Your Potential and Finding True Happiness
Robertson Publishing – 2018

Above All Else –
A Year of Increasing Wisdom, Stature, and Favor
Eagle Rise Speakers Bureau– 2018

The Good Soldier
How to Fight Well, Finish the Race, and Keep the Faith
Eagle Rise Publishing – 2019

CrossFit® Journal Articles

A Chink in My Armor

Coaching the Mental Side of CrossFit

CrossFit HQ – 2851 Research Park Drive, Santa Cruz, CA.

Diet Secrets of the Tupperware Man Vol. I

Diet Secrets of the Tupperware Man Vol. II

Forging Elite Leadership

Good Housekeeping Matters

How to Grow a Successful Garage Gym

Training Two Miles to Run 100

ACKNOWLEDGMENTS

First and foremost, I am deeply grateful for the everlasting love and embrace of God and His Son, Jesus Christ. For my beloved parents, Raymond and Julianne Amundson, who encouraged me from a young age to develop my mind, body, and spirit in such a manner that I could be of greater service to others. A great deal of appreciation is extended to Brooklyn Taylor for her brilliant layout and design contributions to this book. I am also indebted to the plank owners of the Patriot Authors Network and Eagle Rise Speakers Bureau: Robert Vera, Josh Mantz, Jay Dobyns, Jason Redman, Kevin Briggs, and Karen Vaughn. Your true "Warrior Monk" spirit continues to inspire me more every day.

VICTORY!

DEDICATION

*"Children, obey your parents in everything,
for this pleases the Lord."*
— Colossians 3:20

This book is dedicated in loving memory
to my mom and dad, who provided me with the greatest
example of a "Heart like Christ" I have ever known.

_____

*"God is more worthy of your pursuit, attention, and love than all the
other passions of the world combined."*
— Dr. Raymond Amundson

_____

"God is entirely devoted to your personal advancement."
— Julianne Amundson

A NOTE TO THE READER

The Bible says, "the steps of a righteous person are ordered by the LORD" (Psalm 37:23). I believe, therefore, that in the context of my book *Victory*, we were destined to meet in this exact time and place.

This also leads me to believe that you are a warrior. Deep in your soul, God implanted a desire for you to be a vessel of service to other people. Your ability to serve others is contingent upon your drive to first master yourself.

This book will support you on the sacred journey of self-mastery in the service of others, and walking the noble path of a modern day warrior.

Greg Amundson

Santa Cruz, California, 2019

CONTENTS

SYMBOLISM

*"God is your protecting shield
and your triumphant sword."*

—Deuteronomy 33:29

FOREWORD BY ROBERT "THE GHOST" GUERRERO

I have been around the sport of professional boxing my entire life. Oftentimes in this sport, trainers and coaches make their living by *telling* the boxer what to do. They conceive of drills, hold stopwatches, give feedback, design workout programs, prepare nutrition plans, and critique performance.

Greg Amundson is not that type of coach or leader.

From the moment I met Greg, he demonstrated a Christian virtue that was critical to the life of Jesus Christ. Rather than telling me what to do, Greg joined together with me in the training, and demonstrated through his actions the biblical model of leadership that I refer to as, "Come, follow me!" (Reference Matthew 4:19.)

Something that Greg has really helped me see within the pages of the Bible is that God loves His warriors. This has been encouraging to me, and has affirmed in my thinking that God created me with certain skills, abilities, and unique talents that allow me to excel in boxing. I think of myself as a warrior for God, much like King David did when he faced the giant Goliath in single combat.

In my boxing career, I have faced numerous Goliath's. However, even outside the ring, my family and I have faced our share of challenges. Greg's book *Victory* will inspire you to face your own challenges and Goliath's with the heart of a warrior. He provides a roadmap for you to achieve self-mastery in the service of others and to fight (and win!) the good fight of faith.

Be strong and courageous in the Lord!

Robert "The Ghost" Guerrero
Six Time World Champion Professional Boxer

INTRODUCTION

Welcome to *Victory*, my integrated and holistic approach to achieving and maintaining fitness for an eternity. My goal is to provide you with a fully integrated training program that will strengthen your mind, body, and spirit, with an emphasis on achieving the victory both during your time on Earth, and your eternal lifetime in Heaven.

The book is divided into three parts: Part One is the foundation. It focuses on mindset and the productive use of thoughts and words.

Part Two concerns strengthening the spirit, with an emphasis on meditation, breath practices, and spiritual disciplines.

Part Three is devoted to building your body and includes a nine-week training plan that "yokes" the mind, spirit, and physical training into a seamless program designed to accelerate you into the best shape of your life.

You are standing at the starting point of a training program unlike anything else in the world. Your legacy starts today!

WHAT IS *"FITNESS FOR ETERNITY?"*

Several years ago, I came across two Bible verses that radically shaped my life. The context and background for the first verse is important, especially considering a large part of the book you hold in hand is dedicated to developing the strength of your physical body. At the anointing of King David (when David was still a shepherd and several years before he faced Goliath in single combat), God told the Prophet Samuel, "Although people look at the outward appearance, the LORD looks at the heart" (1 Samuel 16:7). In other words, David was anointed by Samuel not for his robustness, strength, or physical stature–*but rather for the quality of his heart.*

This verse serves to encourage an integrated approach to training, with specific practices to strengthen the "heart" by which the biblical author meant the quality and intimacy of our relationship with God. "Fitness for eternity" implies doing everything we can to achieve health, strength, and wellness during the temporal life we enjoy on Earth, in addition to the eternal life we will enjoy in Heaven.

The second verse which greatly influenced the manner in which I started to approach my daily CrossFit® workouts, martial arts, yoga, and fitness training, comes from the Apostle Paul: "The body is a temple for the soul" (1 Corinthians 6:19). The impact of this Scripture in my life has been immense and has inspired me to see that the long-term and eternal benefits of a fitness program are far more important than my "score on the whiteboard" or how I look in the mirror.

The Apostle Paul's "Holy Spirit" insight has motivated me to realize that the totality of my body, including my mind and spirit, are the dwelling place of God's Spirit within me. When this biblical principle is completely understood and obeyed, the only logical way to approach an exercise routine is through an integrated and holistic fitness program that ensures our "temple" is being developed to its fullest potential.

THE VICTORY PHILOSOPHY OF TRAINING WAS BORN

In my experience, the Bible verse, "Seek first the Kingdom of God, and everything else will be added to you" (Matthew 6:33), has immense application within an integrated training program. Based on the reports of the thousands of athletes I have coached, mentored, and trained, I can now confidently proclaim that when we seek to develop our "true core," which is our spirit—our soul, the very presence of God within us—everything else falls perfectly into place. All the extremities of our life improve, not by our own effort, but through the grace and mercy of God.

In addition to the challenging *physical* disciplines I have in store for you during the next several weeks, I also advocate that you begin to practice specific *spiritual* disciplines. The *integration of the physical with the spiritual* is what sets *Victory* apart from other training programs and ensures that you achieve success and happiness within every area of your entire life. With that in mind, I want to immediately introduce you to two specific spiritual disciplines that will become part of the "daily rhythm" of your upcoming training: breathwork and meditation.

BREATHWORK

It says in the Bible, "The Spirit of God has made me, and the breath of the Almighty gives me life" (Job 33:4). In the *Victory* integrated training program, I will be teaching you the practice of "breathwork" in the form of specialized breathing techniques that will accelerate your spiritual growth.

According to my dear friend and world-renowned breathwork pioneer Dan Brulé, the field of breathwork is a new and revolutionary approach to self-improvement and self-healing established in the ancient wisdom of yoga.[1] Breathwork teaches techniques on how to achieve peak performance, optimum health, deep inner peace, and unlimited potential.

MEDITATION

Scripture teaches us to, "Be still, and know I am God" (Psalm 46:10). I believe one of the most effective ways to experience the embrace of God is silence and stillness in His presence. In *Victory*, I will teach you a variety of meditation practices, including the mantra meditation of "I AM" (also taught in my bestselling book, *The Warrior and The Monk*), in addition to meditation on the breath. Both practices have been shown to provide numerous benefits, including a heightened sense of tranquility, mental clarity, peacefulness, and awareness of God's presence.

STAY THE COURSE

I believe in you and in your ability to succeed. I promise that if you stay the course for the duration of the *Victory* training program, your life will never be the same. I'm here to be your guide, mentor, and coach. By developing micro-goals, a positive mental attitude, and proper nutrition, combined with the character qualities of perseverance, determination, and faith, you'll be well on your way to the best shape of your entire life. But before we get started, I want to share a little of my history with you.

A LITTLE HISTORY

I was blessed from a very young age with an appreciation for holistic fitness. Some of my earliest childhood memories involve going to the local YMCA with my dad and working out together. The workouts focused on the basics of gymnastic movements, including handstands, push-ups, dips, and pull-ups. Technique, range of motion, and composure in these skills were ingrained in me. I learned to value the effort that went into developing strength.

Even at a young age, the idea was forming in my mind that the same willpower I was using to conjure up the effort to perform one more pull-up could be used in the classroom to solve the math equation that had been challenging me. Furthermore, mainly because my dad was a doctor of chiropractic, Christian minister, and former naval officer, the idea of alignment between the body, mind, and spirit captivated my imagination and set me on a lifelong journey of pursuing higher levels of living.

Shortly after my dad passed away from cancer, I had the once-in-a-lifetime opportunity to meet and begin a student-teacher relationship with Coach Greg Glassman, the founder of CrossFit. The timing of our meeting was divinely appointed: at a time in my life when I needed leadership and a mentor to continue where my dad had left off, "Coach" came into my life. His leadership, wisdom, passion for teaching, and brilliance for forging elite human performance was exactly what I needed at that moment in my life.

In 2001, I was a newly sworn deputy sheriff in the Santa Cruz County Sheriff's Office and well aware that physical fitness was absolutely critical in my job performance and could literally mean the difference between life and death. Less than a month before meeting Coach and beginning my journey in CrossFit, I had a horrific fight while trying to apprehend a wanted parolee. My greatest enemy during the melee turned out to be my own exhaustion. By the time my backup arrived, I could hardly breathe.

That incident prompted my experimentation with harder and more austere levels of fitness training, my goal being to recreate the levels of exhaustion, stress, fear, and anxiety I had faced on the street.

It wasn't until my first CrossFit workout, laid out in a heap in a corner of the gym, wondering if I was going to live, that I said to myself, "This is what I've been looking for!"

That journey began in December of that year, after becoming intrigued by rumors of athletic monsters being created inside a small gym on the east side of Santa Cruz. My good friend Sam Radetsky had found the number for CrossFit in the Yellow Pages and encouraged me to call. After a few rings, a now-familiar voice answered, "Hello!" In the background I heard grunting, cheering, and the sound of heavy objects slamming against what I hoped was the ground and not any other immovable objects. I introduced myself and asked if I could visit the gym to check things out. None other than CrossFit founder Greg Glassman answered, "Sure, show up tomorrow morning at 6 a.m. and be ready to work out."

I had recently graduated from the University of California at Santa Cruz, where I competed in NCAA water polo. Following graduation, I was hired as a recruit deputy with the sheriff's office and was now fresh out of the South Bay Regional Police Academy. My fitness training up to that point had mainly been aquatic-based with a combination of dry-land gymnastics movements, such as pull-ups and dips. Free weights were available at the university gym and I occasionally performed the bench press and back squat. The police academy, on the other hand, had focused on long-distance running and various defensive-tactics drills. I was young and competitive and thought I was physically fit. I was about to discover just how little I knew.

I pulled into the six-car parking lot in front of CrossFit about 5:45 a.m. that next day. I had been in and around fitness gyms my entire life but something didn't feel right about this one. I was staring at a twelve-foot-tall garage door, the window of which was already fogged up from the inside with moisture and perspiration despite the cold ocean air.

I knocked before entering the small garage and then stepped inside the black-matted room. With a huge smile on his face, Glassman walked across the floor and reached out his hand. "Glad you made it! You can call me Coach," he said.

Seated on what looked like two wooden beams (I would later learn this was a set of gymnastics parallel bars) was the fiercest-looking man I had ever seen. "Greg, meet Mike Weaver, a jiu-jitsu wizard and CrossFit stud. I'm going to have you two workout against each other," Coach said. I had never heard of a jiu-jitsu wizard and I had never worked out "against someone" but I was certain I did not want Mike to show me what either one was.

Coach introduced me to the structure of the upcoming workout. It consisted of a one-thousand-meter row on a Concept2 rower, which Coach claimed was the best piece of "cardio" equipment in the world. Following the row, I would complete twenty-one kettlebell swings and twelve pull-ups. If I felt up to it, he said I could repeat the workout after a brief rest. In the back of my mind, I thought, "Well, that doesn't seem too hard. This should only take me a few minutes!"

Before the workout started, Coach led me from one station to the next, explaining and demonstrating the points of performance and the expected range of motion for each exercise. While receiving Coach's instruction and practicing the skills, I watched out of the corner of my eye as Mike warmed up with some pull-ups. After carefully observing a few of Mike's repetitions, my first thought was, "Man, he is cheating!" Mike was using his legs and hips in a manner that seemed to accelerate his body and almost float his chin over the bar. I was basing my critique of Mike's technique on the strict California Police Academy rules I had been under as a recruit and a historic belief that the pull-up was a biceps exercise.

After a few repetitions at each station under the watchful eye of Coach, we were ready for the start of the workout. Coach explained to me what Mike already knew: CrossFit workouts were, by their design, competitive. Mike and I would be racing against each other and against the clock.

Coach led Mike and me to the second-story landing of the small but immaculately kept gym, where two Concept2 rowers sat side by side, then said, "You guys will row up here, then carefully walk down the stairs to the remaining two stations." "Walk *carefully*? I wonder why he said that," I thought to myself.

Coach then said four words that would soon become as distinctive as legendary boxing announcer Michael Buffer's "Let's get ready to rumble!" catchphrase: "Three...two...one... Go!" Coach thundered, and I started to pull as hard as I could on the handle of the Concept2 rower. A mere three hundred meters into the workout, I knew I had greatly underestimated the impact such a seemingly harmless piece of "cardio" equipment could have on my entire body.

After finishing the row, I also understood why Coach had warned us to walk carefully down the stairs. My legs felt like spaghetti noodles and I had to support myself on the railing as I walked to my next station. Coach enthusiastically motivated and supported Mike and me through the swings and onto the pull-up bar. Mike used a skill I would later learn was the "kipping pull-up" to quickly perform twelve consecutive pull-up repetitions. I, on the other hand, still considered this cheating and, instead, performed three sets of four strict pull-ups.

After the workout—I only completed one round—I stumbled over to the corner of the gym near the stairs and collapsed. Physically, I was finished but internally, I was vibrant with the realization I had discovered something sacred. I had found a coach who would share with me the Holy Grail of fitness.

Over the next several years, I was immensely blessed to be under the guidance of such world-class athletic and spiritual mentors, many of whom I feature throughout the book. They include: Mike Burgener (founder of the CrossFit Olympic lifting trainer course), Jeff Martone (founder of the

CrossFit kettlebell trainer course), Brian MacKenzie (founder of the CrossFit endurance course), Jeff Tucker (founder of the CrossFit gymnastic trainer course), Mark Divine (founder of SEALFIT, Unbeatable Mind, and Kokoro Yoga), Dan Brulé (world-renowned breathwork master), Londale Theus (former SWAT operator with the Santa Monica Police Department and lead Krav Maga FORCE training instructor), John Hackleman (founder of The PIT martial arts), Rolf Gates (world-renowned yoga and meditation teacher), Raja John Bright (a personal student of Maharishi Yogi), Chaplain Richard Johnson (a thirty-year law-enforcement chaplain), and the incredible seminary professors of Western Seminary.

Coach Glassman and the other remarkable mentors, guides, and coaches were each uniquely responsible for teaching me the principles that ultimately shaped my understanding of a holistic, integrated, and congruent mind-body-spirit training system.

In addition to the athletic, yoga, spiritual, and mindfulness coaches I studied and trained with, through my unique experiences in the US Army, as a special agent with the Drug Enforcement Administration (DEA), and as a SWAT operator with the Santa Cruz County Sheriff's Office, I was richly blessed to receive mentorship from world-class warriors. To provide for my warrior-mentors safety, I will not mention their names here but trust me when I say that these men and women were instrumental in teaching me that when physical strength departs the body it's the mind and spirit which take over and allow success both on and off the battlefield.

It's the totality of these lessons that I now share with you in my *Victory* integrated training program.

PART ONE
THE MIND

PART ONE: THE MIND

THE NATURE OF THE MIND

In the early days of CrossFit, Coach told me after a particularly grueling workout that, "Men will die for points." He was referring to the "score on the whiteboard," which my fellow training partners and I had just worked so hard to achieve. However, despite how hard I had worked, at the end of the day, a spray-bottle of Windex and damp towel would erase the scoreboard and the unsuspecting eye would have no clue the battle that had taken place.

The Apostle Paul used athletic training as an analogy for spiritual discipline on numerous occasions. For example, in his letter to the Church of Corinth, Paul wrote, "I do not run like someone running aimlessly; I do not fight like a boxer beating the air" (1 Corinthians 9:26). He knew his "score" was not a temporal matter; rather, it was a matter of eternity and of the Kingdom of God. I think Paul also understood the relationship between the quality of our thinking and the resulting health of our body and life circumstances.

I've discovered that although physical training is extremely important, the real results both in the gym and in life are directly related to the perpetual thoughts we entertain on a daily basis. In the same manner that we must understand the nature of the body in order to strengthen it, we must understand the nature of the mind in order to train it to work for us rather than against us.

The majority of the great spiritual texts and disciplines teach that the fundamental cause of suffering is the mind's tendency to regress to the past or project itself into the future. The solution, therefore, is to discipline the mind to remain centered in the present moment. During meditation, this tendency of the mind to leap out of the present moment becomes extremely apparent. Holding the attention on the present moment can seem harder than the most demanding physical workout. In many respects, learning to "work in" is more challenging—and more important—than learning to "work out." As my good friend and longtime mentor Mark Divine once told me, "The final frontier is not outer space but is, rather, inner space."

Reflecting on my military and law enforcement career, I found how easy it was for my mind to project itself into the future and worry about what might happen. Because my mind was resting on a future creation that had no bearing in the present moment, I would be unaware of my body and my breathing. As a result, my body was tight and my breathing shallow, which only further exasperated the mental sensations I was entertaining.

Learning to remain present, with the mind continually realigning to the body and the breath, is an extremely powerful practice that can have a profoundly positive effect on your life. This ability to remain present is the beginning of your spiritual practice. Remaining present helps you gain perspective on what is permanent and what is temporary. And most of the time, the problem we are focusing on is our *perception* of a situation and not the situation itself. It's our thinking that determines the quality of what we are seeing.

A childhood story will help elaborate on the power of the mind and the importance of properly managing our thoughts. When I was in seventh grade, I was beat up by a school bully named Devon. Devon beat the heck out of me because, unbeknownst to me, I had made a flirtatious remark to a beautiful eighth grade girl named Rebecca in the school lunch line. It seemed I had failed to get the memo that Rebecca was, according to Devon, *his* girlfriend.

So, there I am, standing with many of my friends on the lawn waiting for my mom to pick me up and, suddenly, a group of eighth-graders started to circle around me—one of whom was Devon. He pinned me against a tree, kneed me in the groin, elbowed me in the chest, then the neck, and finally the head; the whole time, screaming in my face, "Man, if I ever see you talking to my girlfriend again, I'm going to whip your ass."

Believe me when I say that he whipped it pretty good that day and I certainly didn't want another ass-whipping in the future.

There were so many layers to the despair that I experienced that moment. One was being unable to defend myself. I was so severely unprepared for Devon's level of strength, aggression, and violence, in addition to the severity and speed of the onset of the attack. In other words, I was caught completely unaware.

The second great despair was a feeling of betrayal. As this was unfolding, I recall looking to my friends for help and they were just as terrified as I was.

Rather than coming to my rescue, they ran away! They wanted no part of that beating. So, as if it wasn't bad enough that I couldn't protect myself, neither could I count on my friends for help. Furthermore, there are all the other layers of ego identification; the ego-bruising that takes place, the feeling that my pride was lost, and the feeling of embarrassment. On and on it went—my thinking about the incident was quickly spiraling out of control.

When I finally got home that afternoon, I eagerly awaited the arrival of my dad—a bodybuilder and martial artist. So, I thought to myself, "This is great. I'm going to learn from my dad tonight how to defeat that bully." My thoughts were of revenge, "Give me a couple of weeks, Devon. I'm coming for you, man. You better watch out."

When my dad finally got home, I went right up to him and explained the entire story. I really hoped he would begin the martial art training immediately. After all, there was a strong likelihood I would see Devon again the next day. Instead, what my dad said was, "Well, the next time that happens, just turn the other cheek. Greg, never resist force with force. Never resist violence with violence." He got out the Bible and conducted a Bible study with me on the lesson of nonviolence with Jesus Christ.

The next morning over breakfast, my dad said to me, "You know, Greg, I will teach you how to defend yourself. Everyone needs to know how to achieve a certain degree of self-protection from harm. Everyone needs to know that. Yet if I find out that you used violence against this person, I will be really, really sad. I'll feel that you would have missed the lesson. Because, the best way to ensure that you never ever have to experience the effect of a bully again is to change your thinking about what happened."

And that is when it hit me. That's when I understood. That's when I began to realize that the physical pain of the assault was done and over with. In fact, it didn't physically hurt very much to begin with. What hurt was my thinking that it was going to happen again and the idea that my friends weren't going to like me anymore because they saw me get beat up. What hurt was my thinking, "How am I going to face Rebecca again? What am I going to say to her now that she knows that I got beat up?"

What hurt was my *thinking*. It was causing me pain and a great deal of it, at that. And what my dad taught me was that if I could change my thinking, I would cease to attract another condition that had unfolded the day before.

Now, this is a fairly advanced concept for a seventh-grade boy to understand. And even to this day, I'm still doing my very best to understand the teachings of Jesus Christ, which is that everything that we experience in our life begins in our mind. In many respects, we are all architects of our lives and the building blocks that we have at our disposal are our thoughts. That's what it boils down to. And that is exactly what my dad taught me that day.

As I grew older, I began to take more and more interest in my dad's profession—chiropractic care—and the relationship between thinking and health. My dad explained to me that the human body was a perfect creation and, as such, we were divinely entitled to a life of perfect health and wellness. He explained illness by saying that the only thing capable of preventing that perfection from manifesting in any area of our lives was misalignment. In other words, people are sick because they are not in alignment with the truth of who they are.

For years, my dad's understanding of the adjustment was only on the physical level. When I would go into his office and watch him adjust patients, I was always amazed that he could put his hands on a patient and by applying very specific pressure to a vertebrae on that person's spine, he could return them to health. I thought that my dad was a miracle worker!

In the course of time, something began to shift in the way my dad adjusted his patients as a direct result of his increasing faith in the healing potential of God and his greater understanding of the power of the mind. As he began to deepen his understanding of those two things, he began to gravitate away from mere physical adjustment and, instead, focus on a mental and spiritual adjustment.

To that end, he would pray for his patient just before going into the adjustment room. He would pray not only for the physical health of the patient but also for their mental health. And as he gained an even greater understanding of the mind's power, my dad would pray for the mindset of the patient—that the patient's mind would radiate with thoughts of health and wellness. Once that prayer was said, he would go into the room and provide a manual adjustment.

The number of adjustments he would give, however, was far less than it had been a few years prior. And as his journey continued, as his relationship with God continued to grow, and as he gained a greater understanding of the power which we all possess to heal ourselves and each other, he entirely ceased to lay hands on the patient. It was simply the prayer followed by his presence in the room with the patient that restored health.

When my dad passed away, more than two thousand people came to Presentation Church in Stockton, California to pay their respects. The majority of them I never knew. And here's what's really amazing: many of those who came to pay their respects had never personally met my dad; they were the sons and daughters, husbands and wives, and friends of my dad's patients. They came to pay their respects because my dad had taught them the power of right thinking. He had instilled in them the Word of God and when we become filled with the Word of God, we naturally have an aspiration to share it and teach it to others. In many respects, this book is a perfect example of that. I'm simply continuing to share with you what my dad shared with me.

As a young boy, I once asked my dad to explain chiropractic adjustments to me. He said, "Son, sometimes you have to be a little cracked to let the light in." As anyone who's received an adjustment knows, it is often accompanied by an audible "cracking" sound. According to my dad's faith and his understanding of the human body, that crack lets the light of God in.

As my dad's journey in the chiropractic profession matured, the "crack" he offered people had far less to do with a physical adjustment and more to do with a mental and spiritual adjustment. When we crack open our old ways of thinking, a new and right spirit can be formed within us. The presence of God can enfold our soul. We can be lifted to the highest realms possible.

BREATHING

The Book of Genesis tells that God took the dust of the Earth and formed the body of man, then breathed into the nostrils of man the breath of life, and the man became a living soul (Genesis 2:7). Meditation on this biblical account of creation has led me to understand that before God breathed the breath of life into our soul, we were simply a body. Yet, in the moment that God breathed His breath into our lungs, we awoke. We became fully integrated. The mind, the body, and the soul were all integrated through the breath of God.

One of the most gifted athletes I have ever had the pleasure of training with is named Robert Guerrero. He's known in the boxing community as "The Ghost" and is one of the best boxers in the entire world (Robert is a six-time, multi-weight division world champion). When he and I train together for his upcoming fights, we train incredibly hard. In fact, it often reminds me of my early days on the CrossFit Level I certification tour, when I would not be able to sleep the night before a course due to the inevitable clash with the workout "Fran" that Coach Glassman would demand of me the following day.

When Robert enters his training camp (a fighting term for the five to seven weeks of intense training leading up to a fight), we train together Monday through Saturday. Every Sunday, we attend church together at Foothills Church in Gilroy, California. One day in church, there was a song the choir was singing. Now, I'd heard this song before. I am obviously familiar with the Bible verse this song is based upon; I just shared it with you from the Book of Genesis. Yet what we often need is the right circumstance, the right environment, the right context for a message to be fully grasped and understood. And there was something about that day in church, standing next to Robert, singing this song—it dawned on me the power and the greater implication of this Bible verse for the modern-day warrior. The song goes:

"It's your breath in our lungs,
So we pour out our praise,
We pour out our praise.
It's your breath in our lungs,
So we pour out our praise
To you only, God."

That song runs like background music in my mind every time I work out. It's the same for Robert. Think of the greater implications of that song and that Bible verse. Every time you draw in a deep breath, that's the breath of God in your soul, my friends. What power you possess through the breath of God. It's not that you're breathing in; it's that God is breathing into you. Wow!

Understanding the breath, maximizing the effectiveness of the breath, essentially becoming—as my dear friend Dan Brulé, author of *Just Breathe: Mastering Breathwork for Success in Life, Love, Business and Beyond*, says— we need to become a "lover of our breath." Of course, there's so much to love because that's the breath of God flowing into our minds, into our hearts, into our souls, into every cell of our bodies.

In Chapter 14 of my book, *Firebreather Fitness,* I dedicate an entire section to investigating the power that we all possess every time we breathe in and breathe out. That power is there whether or not we're even aware of it. The beauty of the breath is that, remember, the presence of God is always there regardless of if we perceive it or not. Therefore, as we develop awareness of the breath, we simultaneously begin to develop awareness of God.

The breath allows us to fully integrate the very presence of God, especially when every breath in which we partake resonates with us at the deepest level of the fact that that is the breath of God flowing into every cell of our bodies.

Breathing can be a spiritual practice that helps cultivate your ability to meet and greet stress in the present moment as it arises in your consciousness. Engaging stress as a warrior means dealing with it on the field of battle at the moment the stress presents itself. In this context, the stress can turn into a strengthening experience and an opportunity to discipline yourself to remain in the present moment. Breathing is one of the most valuable tools you have at your disposal to help you do just that. The practice of monitoring your breath teaches stability. It also helps the mind discover what action can be taken in the present and what your illusions of the future—or memories of the past—may need to be resolved or perhaps, more importantly, forgiven.

A yoga teacher instructs the student to bring awareness to the four parts of the breath. Here's where it really gets exciting and where we really develop the warrior's ability to understand the power of the breath. Every time you breathe in, even though you may not be aware of it, there are four distinct moments that transpire because there are four distinct parts of every breath that you take: the inhalation, the retention of the breath after inhalation, the exhalation, and the suspension of the breath after exhalation.

Now, let's look closer at these four parts of the breath and the quality that determines the benefit of each of these distinct moments.

The inhalation should be long, slow, subtle, and deep, and should evenly spread throughout the entire body. Isn't that beautiful? Imagine that every breath that you take in is evenly spreading throughout every cell of your body. And remember that every breath in is the breath of life, the breath of God flowing into your body. There's no need to rush the inhalation. Instead, savor the duration of every inhalation that you take. The in-breath draws energy from the atmosphere into the cells of the lungs and rejuvenates and restores the life force within you. By retaining the breath once it's drawn in, the energy is fully absorbed and evenly distributed throughout all systems of the body through the circulation of the blood.

The slow release of air during the exhalation carries out and removes accumulated toxins, both mental and physical. By pausing after the out-breath to a level of comfort unique to every moment, all mental stresses are purged and the mind is naturally drawn to the present moment as a result. Continue to draw your attention to the inner movement of the breath and become sensitive to each of the four parts of the breath. It essentially becomes impossible for your awareness to remain attached to the external senses, the past or the future, because you are so absorbed with every moment of the breath.

Even one breath—this is the key insight—taken in absolute present-moment awareness is enough to release the grasp of the past or the tempting illusion of the future.

Meditation on the breath is a powerful step in the withdrawal from the external engagement of the mind with the memories of the past or the tendency to plan, wrestle with, or even be remotely concerned for the future. The power of the breath is absolutely amazing. It is one of the greatest tools for the modern-day warrior.

I was featured on the *Veterans Take Charge* radio show not long before writing this book. It was an amazing experience and what made it so profound was the gentleman with whom I was featured on the program with, Joshua Mantz, the author of a book I highly recommend titled, *Beauty of a Darker Soul.*

Josh is one of the most amazing warrior-leaders our country has ever seen. He was a platoon leader in Iraq when he was hit by a sniper's bullet. He was clinically dead for fifteen minutes. But he came back to life, had a miraculous recovery, then volunteered to go back into combat and finish his tour of duty with his men. He now travels all around the nation, teaching the principles of the modern-day warrior, which have more to do with the mind and the spirit than with the physical body. Indeed, Josh embraces the principle working *in* rather than focusing on working *out*.

Josh and I stood side by side, being interviewed on *Veterans Take Charge*, and where do you think the conversation diverted to? The power of the breath. Josh said that through his healing experience, which continues to this day, the greatest asset that he has—the greatest tool, the greatest friend, the greatest companion that Josh embraces on a day-to-day basis—is the breath.

The question that often comes up when I travel and teach is the same question that Josh encounters in his travels, teaching the power of the breath: "What constitutes a breathing practice?"

I posed that question to none other than the breath master himself, Dan Brulé. I asked how much time each day I should devote to my breath practice. I told Dan that I knew approximately how much time I should be investing into my CrossFit workout, my martial arts training, and my yoga practice, and that I felt I understood how much time I should be spending in meditation, communion, prayer, and intimacy with God. But how much time should I spend on my breathing practice? Dan said, "Greg, it's really simple, brother. All you need to take is one mindful breath a day. One mindful breath taken every single day for the rest of your life constitutes a complete breathing practice."

Isn't there some peace in that? What I'm proposing is that you take one mindful breath a day with full awareness and passionate commitment. If that breath that you take in becomes an opportunity for you to experience the very presence of God flowing into every cell of your body, that in and of itself constitutes a complete breath practice.

Thus, we can begin to see the genius of all the great spiritual texts and historical practices in welcoming and inviting a breathing practice. The breath essentially becomes the moment of integration between the mind, the body, and the soul. It anchors us to the present moment. It rejuvenates the body. It restores the tranquility of the mind. It also allows the awareness of God to resonate in the forefront of our consciousness; we gain intimacy, communion, and a present-moment awareness of the presence of God with every breath we take when it is taken with mindfulness, concentration, and complete and utter awareness.

When we tap into the great witness within us and when that great witness is fully aware of the breath, we achieve the peace and the presence of God.

With that in mind, I want to teach you about a breathing technique that has some unique history in my life. I first learned this technique from one of the most amazing modern-day warrior scholars in the world: Col. Dave Grossman, retired Army Ranger and author of the profound books, *On Combat* and *On Killing.*

When I was assigned to the Drug Enforcement Administration (DEA) Academy in Quantico, VA., as a new DEA special agent trainee, I had the unique opportunity to attend a lecture being given by David. What he proposed to the class that day was that the modern-day warrior needed to learn how to breathe. He posed this question: "Do you know how to breathe?"

And of course, I thought to myself, "I'm a CrossFit athlete, former SWAT operator, and military officer. Of course, I know how to breathe." And undoubtedly, that's what all the other young agent trainees were thinking.

What I came to realize is that the power of the breathing practice that Col. Grossman taught me on that day is one of the foundational breathing practices that most of the modern-day breathing experts teach though it's known by different names.

During the lecture, David explained the breathing practice he coined as, "combat breathing," which was a four-count breathing exercise that helped calm the mind and trigger the body's parasympathetic nervous system. This system, referred to as "rest and digest" is an important contrast to the predominant sympathetic nervous system that most law enforcement and military operators tend to exist in.

The sympathetic nervous system, referred to as the "flight or fight" prepares the body for survival. This system is absolutely necessary during moments when we have to physically protect ourselves, or another person, from a very real threat against our personal safety. However, due to the power of the mind, we can unintentionally remain fixed in this state if we are worrying about the future or trying to change something that's happened in the past. The "combat breathing" technique centered the mind in the present moment and resulted in an increased state of relaxation, mental calm, and focus.

Although I enjoyed the material on the day of the lecture, I did not continue to practice the technique, and soon forgot the important lesson he had provided me. Some years later, another great warrior-scholar—none other than Navy SEAL Commander Mark Divine—would pose to me the same question.

I was at Kokoro Camp in Encinitas, California (a fifty-hour full-immersion camp designed by Mark, intended to replicate the effects of the SEAL's Hell Week). At some point during the first ten hours of the brutal non-stop calisthenics and cold-water immersion, Mark presented this now-familiar question: "Do you know how to breathe?" And thankfully, I said to myself in that moment, "I've got no clue how to breathe. I must need some help because the universe is posing this question to me again."

Mark taught my boat crew the fundamentals of breathing, which was, incidentally, the same technique taught by David. Mark refers to this breathing technique as "box breathing" (Dan Brulé refers to it as "spiritual breathing" and when I teach it, I refer to it as "warrior breathing"). In law enforcement, when you learn the same lesson twice, we call that a *clue*.

I decided to pay attention this time and committed myself to the daily practice of box breathing. I discovered within just a few weeks of practicing the technique an increased sense of inner peace and ability to remain present, even during the stress of a tough physical workout or dangerous mission with the DEA.

I advocate utilizing the nostril breath, which has three significant and additional benefits: the hair follicles in the nose help to either warm or cool the breath before it enters your lungs, depending on which suits the body's needs; the nostrils tend to pull the breath into the lower diaphragm, filling the lungs from bottom to top; it also triggers the parasympathetic nervous system, essentially communicating to your brain to rest and eliciting the emotions of tranquility, peace, and ease.

BREATHING TECHNIQUE: BOX BREATHING

Box Breathing is simple to learn and to begin using right now (breathe through your nostrils). Inhale through the nose. Two... three... four. Hold the breath. Two... three... four. Exhale through the nose. Two... three... four. Hold the breath for another four-count, then slowly and gently release the breath for a four-count. Finally, hold the breath once again for a four-count.

Notice how you feel after four rounds of this form of breathing. This breathing practice is known by different names but follows the same principle, the same methodology, the same system. This is the beginning of your breathing practice. You've just engaged in your first round of box breathing, which may be one of the most important paths that you embark upon on the warrior quest; on the spiritual journey of your life.

Take a moment now to practice box breathing for several minutes. Pay attention to what happens. Notice the dual feeling of stress being melted away and energy being drawn into the lungs and circulated throughout the body. As you gently center you mind on the movement of your breath, notice how you are aligning yourself with the present moment and presence of God.

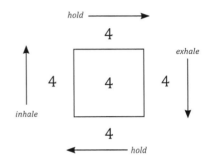

Over the next few days, whenever you feel your temperature rising, like in bad traffic on a freeway, or during a tough *Victory* fitness workout, shift into box breathing mode. Notice what happens. Watch the frustration and anger burn away and the positive energy start flowing in.

ADVANCED BREATHING TECHNIQUE: NADI SHODHANA

The next breathing technique I also learned from Mark Divine. It is a bit more advanced. Think of box breathing as your physical squat: an essential skill that will increase your power in the mental and spiritual realm. The technique that follows is like handstand push-ups and overhead squat: more advanced, yet when practiced and developed, will yield benefits beyond your wildest dreams.

Nadi Shodhana means "alternate nostril breathing." It's a super powerful breathing technique that I practice on a daily basis.

Gently exhale all the air out through both nostrils. Close the right nostril with the thumb of the right hand, and inhale slowly and deeply through left nostril. Close the left nostril with the right ring finger, releasing the thumb, and exhale through the right. Inhale through the right, then close it with the thumb and exhale through the left. This makes one round. Complete ten rounds.

I want to conclude this chapter on breathing with a wonderful story from the warrior tradition that brings to life and enhances what we are trying to accomplish through the breath.

Many, many years ago, a young student of the breath approached his teacher and asked, "Teacher, what am I trying to achieve with the breath? What are the qualities of the breath in my life? How do I know when I am approaching the fruits of the practice? What will the experiences in my life be like as I begin to mature in my breathing practice?"

His teacher replied, "Imagine a rock that is very, very dry. Imagine now that that dry rock has a line carved into it; a line etched into it. A line cut into it. Now, take that rock with the line etched into it and place it at the foot of the seashore. How many years would it take the ocean and the tide and the waves and the sea to wash over that rock before the line that you've etched into the rock was made smooth?"

The student said, "Well, it would take an eternity; it would take years and years and years for that rock to be made smooth."

"Exactly," replied the teacher, "and that rock with the line etched into it represents the student that has not yet begun a breathing practice. And now, imagine that rather than drawing a line in the rock, you draw a line in the sand at the foot of the seashore. Now, how many waves and how many tides would it take for the ocean to smooth out the surface of the sand?" asked the teacher.

The student thought for a moment and then replied, "well, it may only take one tide. In fact, perhaps even one wave could effectively return the sand to its inherent nature of smoothness."

"Yes, you are exactly correct," the teacher replied, "and that is a metaphor for the student who has begun a daily breathing practice. And now imagine," continued the teacher, "you walk out into the ocean and draw a line in the ocean water with your finger. Notice that as you drew the line through the ocean, the water would immediately return to its innate form. This is a metaphor for the student that has made the breathing practice a part of their daily life experience."

"And now," continued the teacher, "imagine that rather than drawing a line in the rock, or in the sand, or even in the ocean, you simply draw a line with your finger through the air. That is a metaphor for the student that has become one with the breath. The breath has become an intimate part of everything they do."

Take a moment to contemplate that story. Which character in the story are you at this moment? Are you the rock? Have you not yet begun a breathing practice? Are you the sand? Are you the ocean? Are you the air?

INTRODUCTION TO MEDITATION

The most simple yet effective techniques to hone strength and resiliency are those aimed at stress reduction. Combating stress in order to relax the body and quiet the mind builds your spiritual strength and aids you in every endeavor of your entire life. The majority of the great spiritual texts and disciplines teach that the fundamental cause of suffering is the mind's tendency to either regress to the past or project itself into the future. The solution, therefore, is to discipline the mind to remain centered in the present moment.

During meditation, the tendency of the mind to leap out of the present moment becomes extremely apparent. Indeed, we find that holding the attention on the present moment can seem harder than the most demanding physical workout. In many respects, learning to work *in* is more challenging and much more important for the modern-day warrior than learning to work *out*.

When we become still and silent and begin to witness our thoughts, we awaken the part of our consciousness I've referred to as "the great witness." This ability to create a little bit of space between our thoughts and our great witness helps us discern where we are focusing our attention.

You see, your mind, it's like a giant magnifying glass, and what you focus on will therefore tend to increase in your life. Let me say that one more time. It's so important, my friends. Your mind is like a giant magnifying glass. And, here's the key, what you focus on will therefore tend to increase in your life. When you focus on a problem, the problem only increases.

The real insight here, as I've pointed out above, is that the problem that we are focusing on is our perception of a situation and not necessarily the situation itself. In other words, it's our thinking that determines the quality of what we are seeing. And when we change the way we look at something, what we look at begins to change. Everything begins in the temple of our mind.

Again, let me reiterate that: if all you took away from this chapter was this particular insight, it would be enough to change your life. It's a nugget of pure gold: our *thinking* determines the quality of what we

are seeing. When we change the way we look *at* something, the thing we're looking at also begins to change.

As you'll see at the end of the book in the nine-week training plan, meditation is part of the drumbeat of your daily workout. In yoga and in the martial arts, meditation is a discipline used to quiet the mind and spend time in a heightened state of awareness of the presence of God. There are more hard-science benefits as well: increasingly, meditation is being used to enhance cognitive performance and reduce the ravaging effects of stress. The news of meditation as a method to improve focus and cognitive performance has a generation of adopters across a wide swathe, from elite military forces to Silicon Valley.

Meditation within the context of the following nine-week plan provides the integrating element that ultimately links the mind, body, and spirit practices together. During mediation, you are able to holistically unite your values and actions while calming the turbulence of your mind. Even just a few minutes of silence and stillness each day can have a resounding effect on the quality of your entire life experience.

One of the best ways to experience the benefits of meditation is to become aware of the subtle internal energy body and to witness the quality of each breath. We tend to think of energy production in the external sense of the term. However, when you become still and silent during meditation, an entirely new world will open before you. You become more aware and sensitive to how closely your thoughts and emotions are linked together.

During the course of the day, we tend to focus on external objects passing through our field of vision. As a result, our energy is drawn out into the world. The tendency of the mind when focusing on the outside world is to attempt to control our environment and resist change. Meditation helps to reverse the tendency of the mind to attach to the external world and to reverse the flow of our life force from the outside to the inside. This is why Jesus Christ taught, "Behold, the Kingdom of God is within you" (Luke 17:21).

The benefits to becoming still and "Seeking God within his Kingdom" are immense and have been the single most important practice in my life. The combination of breathing practices and meditation will be equally powerful and rewarding for you.

During an advanced meditation course with master yoga teacher Rolf Gates, he offered me this visual representation of the effects of meditation, "When you sit down, close your eyes and become still, the sand begins to settle and the water will become clear." In other words, non-action and non-activity allow us to settle down and in this settled state, our minds find clarity.

It is important to note that meditation is not necessarily the absence of thoughts. Meditation is the *returning of the attention to the focus of the meditation*. For example, during meditation, you may choose to focus on your breathing. In this manner, you sit down, close your eyes and become still. You begin to cultivate your witnessing self and watch yourself breathe. You essentially witness yourself take a deep breath in, you witness the moment of retained breath, you witness yourself exhale, then you witness the suspended breath. In the moments that you are absolutely one with present moment of breathing, you are experiencing meditation and a deep sense of peace will be your natural state.

Now, what I just described is often easier said than done. After taking even an initial deep breath in, the tendency of the mind is to immediately wonder, "Did I remember to lock the car?" The mind jumps away from the intended focus of meditation. Rather than judging this experience as negative, your task is to simply return the awareness back to the breath. Rolf put it this way, "Meditation is the constant aligning and realigning of the awareness back to the present moment."

Along with the experience of watching my breath, I employ another meditation technique frequently: the repeating of a mantra within my mind. The mantra is wonderful because it allows the mind to enjoy its natural state of activity in a focused manner. For example, the mind's usual tendency is to jump from thought to thought, idea to idea, memory to memory. By introducing a mantra, the mind settles around this word, repeating it over and over until the thinking becomes more subtle.

In this meditation, it is common to experience internal silence between the thoughts. This is what Deepak Chopra refers to as, "slipping into the gap between your thoughts."[2] The great wisdom teachers instruct that the space between thinking is the universal space of pure awareness. You directly experience the universal mind, pure potentiality, and the unlimited nature of your spirit. Ultimately, meditation will lead you to experience the presence of God.

In yogic meditation, it is common to use the mantra of the sound "*om*" and in my early childhood experience in the Catholic Church, we did something similar.

When I was in first grade at Presentation Elementary School in Stockton, the school—associated with Presentation Catholic Church—was presided over by a senior priest named Father Michael Kelly. From grades one through six, my teachers were nuns. This was a very, very traditional Catholic school. We began every morning with prayer, both silently and as a class, led by either the nun who was teaching us or, on Fridays, we would have a special visit from Father Kelly.

One morning, after we prayed the Lord's Prayer with Father Kelly, he challenged us to repeat in our mind ten times the word "amen." The challenge was repeating the word ten times perfectly clearly in our mind and to count every repetition of the word "amen." In the event we were trying to *think* the word, yet another thought entered our mind, we simply forgave ourselves for not being able to reach ten reps and then went back to the beginning. This process would repeat itself over and over until we were able to count ten repetitions.

Although Father Kelly did not refer to this particular practice as such, that was my first introduction to the power of meditation. It's amazing what he instilled in me that day. The ability to focus the mind on one particular word is known in the meditation practices as *transcendental* or *mantra* meditation. It involves focusing the mind on one word or sound that may not have any meaning whatsoever. We simply repeat the sound or the word over and over and over, and that word or sound acts like an anchor that drops through our consciousness, through our thinking mind into the very depths of our soul. It allows the mind to be still and become clear.

The real joy to be had in meditation is that once the mind becomes still, we can experience the presence and the peace of God.

There's a fantastic story that is told in the warrior tradition of martial arts of a young martial artist who comes to his master instructor and asks, "How do I know when I'm ready?" This young man wants to have some certainty that his technique has reached a level of proficiency which would allow him to defend himself should he be attacked. His teacher promptly sits down in a meditative posture and says, "When you can sit in silent meditation and not the roughest ruffian would dare make onset to your presence, then you're ready."

What I understand now within that story is that the teacher was instructing the student to so cultivate the quality of his mind that it would be at peace. As a martial artist, if we can discipline the mind to be still, we create peace in our environment. This is why in *The Art of War,* Sun Tzu describes the power of becoming still in your mind. He says that to win a thousand battles without fighting is the essence of the true warrior. Win first in your mind, then walk onto the field of battle; for only then, can you always prevail.[3] That is meditation.

I also love that story because it's often we find ourselves assuming that the next accolade, the next physical accomplishment, or the next object of our desire will lead to our happiness and help us feel like we've got it, that now we're ready.

The physical pursuit within the world is so tempting yet, time and time again, the wisdom tradition from the Bible to the martial arts teaches us it is, in fact, our ability to be still both in body and in mind that is the true path; the gateway to all happiness and joy. This is, in fact, why Jesus Christ warned his disciples about the illusion and the temptation of looking over here or looking over there, referring to the tendency of the mind to project itself through the senses onto material objects of our desire. Christ said, "Behold, the Kingdom of God is within you" (Luke 17:21). And it is our practice of meditation that allows us to come into very real contact with the Kingdom of God, with the very presence of God.

The reason that I recommend and endorse meditation is because it works. It has worked tremendously in my life. What I always look for within my circle of mentors are the universal themes, the universal strategies, the universal recommendations that my mentors are making. And what I have found is that every single one of the great mentors in my life, from my father to my early childhood experience with Father Michael Kelly to more recent mentorship with Rolf Gates—a former US Army Ranger—and Mark Divine—a former US Navy SEAL—have taught me the power of stillness.

When I first met each of these men, I was a lot like the student from the story, approaching the great teacher and thinking, "This is the next step on my physical journey. I'm going to learn from these great teachers the practice of yoga." I was associating yoga with Yoga Asana or Vinyasa as we refer to it in the West, meaning the poses of yoga, when, in fact, that was really the last thing these teachers wanted to teach me because they knew I didn't need another physical pursuit. What I needed was to cultivate silence. I needed meditation.

There's a story—as you're no doubt becoming aware, I love stories—that I think offers an interesting perspective on the power of meditation. A young man is walking across a beautiful pristine field when he suddenly encounters an old man. The old man is lying on his back, looking up at the clouds. The young man approaches him and says, "Old man, what are you doing lying on your back here in this pasture?"

The old man replies, "I am watching my thoughts pass by." The young man then says, "It looks like you're watching the *clouds* pass by." The old man replies, "Ha, young man, don't you see? It is the same thing."

This strikes me as the same great witness that Mark Divine and I describe— the great witness in this story is the sky, the thoughts are the clouds passing beneath the awareness of the sky, and what we discover through the practice of meditation is that thoughts come and thoughts go, just like weather comes and goes, just like clouds come and go. And yet, the sky remains the same.

For those of us on the path of the warrior, we discover during meditation that God remains constant. This is why the Bible says God is the same yesterday, today, and forever more (Hebrews 13:8). When our mind settles on the presence of God, we can become still on the rock of His foundation. In that stillness, we then cultivate the ability to watch or witness our thoughts pass by; we discipline ourselves not to attach to the thought. The only way a thought gains power is by our attachment to it or our aversion from it. In and of itself, a thought has no power. We simply breathe life into it when we focus on it.

Meditation has been such a singularly powerful practice in my life and the good news is that the people I am now mentoring and encouraging on the path of the warrior have confirmed the power of that one addition, that one variable in their life: meditation. So, I encourage you, friends, if you have not already started a basic practice of meditation, begin today.

For those who have started on the path of meditation, I offer the advice that one of my drill sergeants gave me in US Army basic combat training: "Stay the course." Commit to your practice of meditation. Just like the practice of breath work, the practice of gaining greater intimacy with the presence of God needs to be a daily discipline. Meditate every day even if it's only for a few moments.

HOW TO WIN IN LIFE

Within just a few months of training with Coach Glassman, I told him I wanted to win every single workout. Winning a workout was equivalent to living or dying on the street. That may sound a little bit extreme. It probably was. However, at that time in my life I was a brand-new deputy sheriff, and to me, winning in the gym was giving me the confidence to win on the street. I simply could not accept anything in the gym other than first place.

So, I went to Coach one morning after taking second place in a workout and said, "Coach, I don't get it. I feel like I'm working physically harder than every single one of these athletes. I'm attending more classes. I'm practicing the physical movements on my own." I was essentially doing double- and triple-day workouts yet, I was not winning the workouts. And I said, "Coach, what do I have to do? Where do I direct my attention?"

I felt certain that Coach was going to spend time with me working on technique and the productive application of strength. Instead, he said, "Kid, what's your nutrition like? How are you eating?"

And what's amazing is at that time, all I could say was, "Well, I'm eating." I really had no awareness. I had no clue as to the quality or the quantity of food that I was putting into my body. Coach basically took sympathy on me and created something of a *Cliff's Notes* of Dr. Barry Sears' book, *Enter the Zone*. He broke it down for me and planned for me a menu that I have altered very little to this day. You see, Coach was the first person that inspired me to understand the power of *physical nutrition*.

The reason I emphasize the word *physical nutrition* is that there is another type of nutrition that is equally important and that is *mental nutrition*. One of the biblical stories I often share in my sermons and lectures is fitting to share here because it is about the power of our mind. The story illustrates how our thoughts ultimately influence the quality of our life experiences.

Jesus Christ was once accused of breaking the sacred law because he did not wash his hands before consuming food. In response, Christ said, "What goes into someone's mouth does not defile them, but what comes out of their mouth, that is what defiles them" (Matthew 15:11).

Isn't that amazing? It is the quality of our spoken word that matters most. And what affects and determines the quality of our spoken word is the quality of our thinking. So, back to meditation, the only way that we can ultimately cultivate a perpetual state of positive and healthy thinking is by allowing our mind to rest in the presence of God.

In the context of meditation, I believe the Bible has a great deal to teach us. For example, consider the incredible implications and argument for the daily practice of meditation hidden within Psalm 51:10: "Create in me a clean heart, O God, and put a new and right spirit within me."

In the following pages, we'll look closer at the exact language that the Bible uses, including its Greek and Hebrew origins, and you'll see that "heart" is the only word of the time to convey a concept still several centuries away from discovery: the subconscious. So, substituting "heart" with "mind," the verse is essentially saying "God, create in me a clean mind. Cleanse my mind, God, of all unhealthy and self-defeating thoughts." And how was the mind to be cleansed? According to the Bible, through the daily practice of meditation, silence, and stillness in the presence of God.

In my Christian daily devotional book, *ABOVE ALL ELSE,* I argue that the repetition of Scripture within our mind leads to a state of tranquility, inner peace, and increasing intimacy with God.[4] In addition, meditation develops the ability to discern the voices within our mind that are serving our greater good, and those voices that are a hindrance to our development and growth. Often during meditation, we come "face to face" with deeply rooted habitual thought patterns that keep us trapped in self-defeating patterns of life experience. How do we escape the voices of self-doubt, anxiety, and fear?

I have found great comfort and healing in the words of Jesus Christ: "But to you who are listening, I say love your enemies, do good to those who hate you, bless those who curse you, pray for those who mistreat you" (Luke 6:27-28). In the context of interpersonal relationships, one of the great lessons Christ taught was to love our enemies. However, what do you do when the enemy you face is your own negative thinking?

Hidden in the rich metaphor of Christ's teaching is the secret to this enduring question. You must discipline your mind to think of love, kindness, forgiveness, and encouragement. In the same manner that a wise carpenter uses a good nail to drive out a bad nail, during meditation you can use a positive thought (or mantra) to replace a negative thought. Jesus taught us not to wrestle with the enemies of discouragement, anxiety, fear, uncertainty, or despair. Instead, he encouraged his followers to call upon the presence of God and elicit the great allies of hope, encouragement, faith, and love.

Isn't that a powerful teaching and insight? This, again, is the benefit of meditation. One of the skills that we develop in meditation is the ability to witness the quality of our thinking, and to replace self-defeating thoughts with thoughts of hope, love, faith, and personal belief.

GOAL-SETTING

The first step in goal-setting is to understand and define our terms in the context of athleticism and personal achievement. For my purposes in this book, I have created a new definition of the word "goal."

> **GOAL:** (noun) 1. A specifically desired end state, expressed in the positive tense, that provides motivation and direction on the path to achievement.

This definition of a goal is unique to the *Victory* program for several reasons. By looking closer at the definition and associated points of performance, we can explore several ways that you can maximize your mind, body, and spirit for an eternity of fitness. In addition to defining our terms, three points of performance in goal-setting will expand upon our definition and ensure your success:

> 1. **The goal must be SPECIFIC:** *"I want to complete 50 gymnastic kipping pull-ups in a single set."*
> 2. **Express your goal in the POSITIVE TENSE:** *"I want to safely perform a backwards roll to support on the rings."* vs. *"I don't want to fall off the rings while upside down."*
> 3. **The goal must include a TIME FRAME** that is challenging yet realistic and achievable.

First, a goal must be specific. This means it should be concise, as well. Before you can start on the path to achievement, you must first understand the desired end state. The more focused the definition, the more opportunity there is for precise planning, preparation, and training. In addition, by specifically defining a goal, you can evaluate with precision when the goal has been met.

Second, a goal must be expressed in the positive tense. In order to maximize human athletic potential and harmonize the mind-body connection, it is imperative to understand the significance and power of positive expression. The conscious and subconscious mind will either promote or inhibit athletic performance. If I tell myself consciously, "I don't want to fall off the climbing rope," my subconscious mind, in fact, hears, "I want to fall off the climbing rope." This is because *the subconscious does not hear the negative tense.* By telling yourself what you *don't* want to manifest, you actually create a blueprint for exactly what you intend to avoid.

The key lesson, therefore, is to keep yourself in a constant state of positive affirmation of your goal's desired end state.

The final point is perhaps the most important but least understood: a goal must contain a time frame that is realistic and achievable while simultaneously providing the athlete with a certain amount of challenge and motivation. A goal set too far in the future will lack the urgency and fail to create the internal fire needed for accomplishment. On the other hand, too short a time frame may lead to discouragement and despair.

When deciding on the time frame for a goal, you must engage in a certain degree of honest self-assessment. For example, if you told me your goal was to perform a single set of fifty pull-ups in three months, I would likely ask you how many consecutive pull-ups you can currently complete. How specifically you answer that question will help me in determining the best approach to supporting the achievement of your goal. If you respond, "I'm not sure how many pull-ups I can do right now," we need to immediately find out. The approach we take to setting a time frame for completing fifty consecutive pull-ups will vary greatly if you're currently capable of doing five pull-ups as compared to forty-five pull-ups.

In setting the time frame for a goal, it's important that you weigh the delicate balance between motivating yourself, while at the same time, ensuring yourself a high likelihood of success. The purpose of goal-setting is, don't forget, for you to achieve your goals! Notice the key word here is "achieve." By defining, working toward, and ultimately, arriving at your desired end state, you can develop the habit and pattern of behavior for personal success that can be applied to anything.

The frequency with which you can set a goal for yourself and reach the desired end state of that goal will, in large part, define your sense of self esteem, intrinsic motivation, and personal capacity. This translates to happiness, health, and an eternity of fitness.

When you implement the lesson of goal-setting in your life, an exciting and rewarding journey suddenly awaits the five-pull-up athlete whose goal is to achieve fifty pull-ups (and maybe this is you): he or she has an opportunity to set and reach several smaller and more immediate goals along the way.

These mini-triumphs will reaffirm your ability to succeed and provide you with motivation and confidence. Obviously, well before you can do fifty pull-ups, you must first do ten, then fifteen, and then twenty pull-ups. Each of these seemingly small increments can, in fact, become a huge milestone and a chance for you to say, "I can achieve that which I set my mind to."

—— THE POWER OF POSITIVE SELF-TALK ——

Several years ago, Coach said a few words to me that I will always remember: "The greatest adaptation to CrossFit takes place between the ears." Greatly influenced by his remark, I set out to become a student of the mental aspects of physical training. Through observation, practice, and research, I discovered something remarkable: the world's best athletes had learned to control and optimize their *self-talk*.[5]

This potent mental skill resulted in their ability to formulate and achieve their goals—both inside the gym and out—with consistency and grace. The natural extensions of their positive self-talk were an optimistic energy, a mental toughness, and an indomitable spirit evident in their physical accomplishments in the toughest of workouts and life circumstances.

I concluded that Coach was indeed correct: the mental adaptation to CrossFit and any physical pursuit (ranging from yoga to martial arts to big-wave surfing) was of critical importance to athletes and coaches hoping to forge elite fitness. Now, nearly twenty years after the seed was first planted, I hope to share the key lessons learned as a result of the spark Coach set inside me.

For fitness coaches and individual athletes (after all, you are always coaching and leading at least one person—and that person is you), understanding and ultimately shaping the way you talk to yourself and set personal goals are extremely important for success both in the gym and in life. Understanding the significance of positive self-talk and realistic goal-setting is just as important as instilling a sense of virtuosity in the foundational movements of a fitness program. Although taught, practiced, and learned inside the gym, these lessons have the potential to move outside the gym and continue doing what the *Victory* program does best: improving the quality of your entire life.

If there is one consistent character trait I have observed in the best athletes from around the world, it is a strong sense of *optimism*. The difficulty of the hard, grueling, and demanding training naturally instills not only physical fitness but also mental fitness. Regardless of the time to completion or the amount of weight used, simply facing the daunting workout puts the other obstacles of life into proper perspective: they are all a lot easier. When you understand that optimism and a positive mental attitude can yield tremendous results inside *and* outside the gym, you will increase your success in every area of your entire life.

As a CrossFit athlete and coach, I have concluded that a positive mental attitude and positive self-talk are paramount in achieving the full potential of human work capacity. Simply stated, you've got to learn how to talk to yourself, as well as to your loved ones. To this extent, I have observed that an athlete is impressionable mentally and emotionally at three distinct times while engaging in a physical workout or challenge:

- The half an hour *before* the workout.
- *During* the workout (perhaps the most receptive time).
- Immediately *after* the workout, depending on alertness and fatigue.

With this in mind, it becomes extremely important to engage in positive reinforcement before, during, and after a workout. The reason for this is that your personal reinforcement, either positive or unintentionally negative, will influence your mind at both the conscious and subconscious levels.

The significance of this lesson was most apparent to me during my first attempt at running one hundred miles in twenty-four hours. At the halfway point, I was joined by a coach/pace-runner who informed me, "Don't think about it but the next fifty miles will be the hardest yet."

This coach had no way of knowing the emotional state I was in and I'm sure he had the best intentions with the comment. However, on the receiving end of this bit of advice, I was left emotionally and mentally devastated. My immediate self-talk thought was crushing: "This is about to get a lot harder."

Moments after the attempted pep talk, I was joined by my friend Mallee, who, having overheard the previous comment, loudly exclaimed, "Greg, you're gonna fly through these next few miles!" My mental and emotional state changed in an instant and I felt a surge of strength that replaced the weakness of only a moment before. My subconscious mind heard "fly" and "few miles." The result was positive self-talk that sounded like, "Just a few more miles. I'm gonna fly!"

During a hard workout or season of life, it is impossible to predict what one small word, statement, or comment your mind will hear, register, and be affected by. Therefore, it is vital that you be aware and respectful of the amount of influence that your thinking and speaking has over your entire life.

In CrossFit, we often say, "Every second counts." I've discovered that in addition to every second counting, every word, and every thought counts too.

Students in CrossFit Level 1 courses are taught to cue athletes with specific and concise statements, such as, "Drive through the heels!" I believe that you must learn to articulate positive reinforcement to yourself with the same skill. When an athlete hears from a coach, "You're doing great! You're going to get a personal record," the athlete internalizes these specific and tactful words and the meaning of the statement. The effect of the coach's words on the athlete's self-talk is this: "I am doing great! I am going to get a PR!" Those few words can motivate tired athletes and help strong performers work just a little bit harder.

In addition to having an awesome effect on other people, speaking in encouraging, supportive, and positive ways to yourself can have a great effect as well.

Legendary fight trainer and longtime mentor John Hackleman taught me the significance of essentially scripting athletes' self-talk for them. John is the founder of The Pit Fight Team and coach of former UFC champion Chuck Liddell. He uses the mantra "NTLP," meaning "No time like the present." I'm a strong believer in the concept. John says, "When you want to do something, when you want to effect change in your life, there is no time like the present."

As a coach, John has used positive reinforcement to help top mixed-martial-arts fighters like Liddell during the one-minute break between rounds of UFC bouts. He explained to me that no matter what had unfolded during the fight up until that point, he would tell the fighter things like, "You look strong. I am proud of you!" and "Your punching is powerful." The focus and word choice always remained in the positive tense.

John said, "I would never say to my fighter, 'You're *not* tired!' or 'You *don't* feel tired' because that would almost guarantee the fighter would walk back into the cage thinking, 'I'm tired' instead of thinking something more productive and positive."

Learning and applying the art of goal-setting and positive self-talk will have an incredible influence on every area of your entire life. The result of practicing these mental skills with the same diligence as your physical skill sets will increase your collective work capacity and sense of personal power both inside and outside the gym. I trust you will reach the same conclusion that I have: what the mind can conceive and believe, the body will achieve.

Former Navy SEAL, Dr. Kirk Parsley, MD, a doctor who specializes in health and performance with active-duty SEALs, gives talks about how performance and willpower are drained if you allow your thoughts to be swept off by insignificant thinking and wasteful decision-making.

Dr. Parsley says that when we wake up in the morning (after a good night of sleep!), we are fully charged with willpower. Our willpower is like a battery that's been fully recharged. However, if the first thing you do is pick up your smartphone and start scrolling through a bunch of junk mail, you're already starting to drain that battery in a wasteful way.

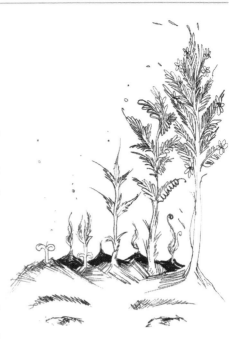

Start your day with a positive mental attitude by developing rituals and what I refer to as a "morning practice" of breathing and meditation.

The morning practice also keeps you in alignment with the words of Jesus Christ, who said, "Seek first the Kingdom of God and everything else will be added to you" (Matthew 6:33). In other words, by making breathing and meditation a priority in the morning, the remainder of your day will be focused and full of passion and purpose to accomplish your big dreams and goals.

Self-talk is a powerful tool to help move you on a steady and productive ascent toward your long-term goals. It is especially important when the course gets challenging, which is sure to take place during the *Victory* nine-week plan.

Timothy Noakes, MD, a renowned sports scientist and author, is largely credited with a theory called the "Central Governor." It looks at the neurobiology of the brain's wiring with regard to discomfort and pain when the body pushes into extremes of exercise. The brain's mechanisms are such that discomfort can be extraordinarily high even though there are still reserves of energy in the muscles. It's as if once you get below a quarter of the gas tank, a computer in the car starts forcing the engine to slow down and even stop. It's a self-protective mechanism.

To get a top-endurance performance out of the body when engaged in a difficult competition, Noakes believes that the moment we allow a negative thought to slip into the internal dialogue—such as, "I'm not sure I can do this," or "I can't keep this up," or "I think I'm going to lose"—the brain chemistry catches wind of this and immediately begins to increase the level of discomfort. Holding the pace or intensity of the effort instantly gets harder.[5]

An example from my experience in the brutal Kokoro Camp will help you understand this principle well. When I was in the forty-first consecutive hour of all-out physical exertion, I found myself struggling with a task of carrying a heavy stone for a matter of hours.

Mark Divine, who ran the camp, saw that I was losing ground and came over to help me get my mind right. It was a heavy rock to begin with and my negative self-talk was making the rock feel much heavier. As I struggled with the rock, Mark asked me, "Which dog are you feeding?"

Mark coaches the principle of positive self-talk using the metaphor of feeding a wolf. As he puts it, at any given moment, your thoughts are either feeding the "wolf of courage" or the "wolf of fear." In fact, I share this fable from the ancient warrior tradition in *The Warrior and The Monk*. Thoughts of positivity and optimism feed the courage wolf. Feeding the wolf of courage makes you feel stronger, more certain of yourself, and helps cultivate an increased sense of personal belief.

Now come with me into the mystical world of *The Warrior and The Monk* ...

"Many years ago, an old sage spoke to a young boy on the evening before he would begin the ritual inauguration into the warrior tradition. The young boy was apprehensive and uncertain of his ability to succeed in the harsh training and conditions that would follow.

The old sage told the young boy,

"There are two wolves engaged in a fierce battle within your mind:

A Wolf of Courage

and...

A Wolf of Fear."

◆◆◆◆

The young boy asked the old sage,

"Which wolf will be victorious in the battle?"

"Whichever wolf you feed," the old sage replied.

"In that case," the young boy thought aloud...

"I must feed the Wolf of Courage."

The old sage then said something that forever shaped the young boy's maturity into the warrior culture...

'The Wolf of Courage and the Wolf of Fear are both starving for your attention, which is governed by your thoughts and words.

A warrior must have...

discipline and willpower to

think and speak positively.

Only positive thoughts and words shall feed the Wolf of Courage."

THE BIBLICAL WOLF OF COURAGE

The Bible says, "As iron sharpens iron, so one person sharpens another" (Proverbs 27:17). This is an awesome verse that carries resounding implications within the warrior tradition. However, in addition to being sharpened and held accountable by another person, it is also important to remember that Scripture teaches God alone is our *ultimate* source of strength, tempering, forging, and sharpening.

The principle of the story is that within our consciousness, a battle is always taking place between the courage wolf and the fear wolf. Because the battle rages within our individual consciousness, we retain influence over which wolf will prevail and the outcome is ultimately determined by the quality of our thinking.

If you're having trouble winning the battle, consider that the Word of God is "useful for correcting and training in righteousness" (2 Timothy 3:1). God designed you in His image, therefore, the Spirit dwelling within you is not weak, timid, anxious, or in any manner congruent with the fear wolf.

Rather, the Holy Spirit within you is a source of "power, love, and self-discipline" (2 Timothy 1:7) that can be your greatest source of strength throughout the various challenges and seasons of your life.

It's time to start feeding the courage wolf by wielding the "sword of the Spirit, which is the Word of God" (Ephesians 6:17).

Try this simple step-by-step process to help feed the courage wolf:

1. **Be aware of your thinking.** As a workout (or life circumstance) grows in intensity, bring increased awareness to the quality of your thinking. Remember that each thought is a piece of "food" and your goal is to feed *only* the wolf of courage.

2. **Prepare for negative thoughts.** If you become aware of a negative thought, take a deep breath in through your nose to create *mental space* for the important next step.

3. **Perform a redirect.** As you exhale, let go of the negative thought and associated energy. On the next inhalation, redirect the energy into a positive image or statement. Use positive statements and words as bits of "mental food" to feed the courage wolf.

This process of awareness, breathing, and redirection is a continual (and beautiful!) process that becomes within itself a profound spiritual practice. What would this process look like for me at that moment in Kokoro Camp? Picture a man who is sleep-deprived, exhausted, soaked head-to-socks from crossing a chilly stretch of salt water, under pressure to get back to the base in a certain amount of time—all while hauling a heavy rock. It's not hard to imagine a negative thought bubbling up like, "I don't think I can do this."

My first task in this case was to be in a state of awareness to catch the thought early like a warrior scout on high alert while navigating across a battlefield. Then, in place of that negative thought, be ready to insert one with a positive emotional charge to it such as, "I've got this!" or other affirmations that focus on making it to the next micro-goal, ensuring that my life energy flows in the right direction. My job was to repeat these positive thoughts one after another, starving the fear wolf and building internal momentum.

This technique has applications toward all sorts of challenging projects and situations: lengthy or intense workouts, running a marathon, studying for finals, preparing for an interview, and so on. Monitor your thoughts, feed your courage, and starve your fear.

Don't be afraid to use the power of the spoken word to intersect and overcome persistent internal negative self-talk. If you are having a hard time internally replacing a negative thought with a positive one, take a deep breath and speak out loud with conviction, energy, and enthusiasm. Hearing yourself speak positively can have a powerful internal effect and help you achieve proper internal self-talk. Sometimes, I shout out in the middle of a workout, "Yes, I can do it!" and I encourage you to do the same.

In August 2018, I achieved a nearly twenty-year goal by obtaining my black belt in Krav Maga. The totality of my test included four grueling days of training that were some of the most challenging physical and mental crucibles of my entire life. On the first day of the test, I crawled back to my hotel room, uncertain how I was going to continue. My body was extremely sore, and I was already covered from head to toe with bruises. In addition to the physical discomfort, I was increasingly aware that my mind was under attack from the wolf of fear.

I said a simple prayer and asked God for help in the upcoming days. I took a few deep breaths, then opened my Bible to the Psalms for a word from God. Through the power of the Holy Spirit, the first Psalm my eyes were drawn to was Psalm 28:7, which reads, "The LORD is my strength and my shield; my heart trusts in him, and he helps me." I was overwhelmed with joy as this particular verse from Scripture fed my courage wolf in a profound way.

Over the next three days, I estimate that I repeated Psalm 28:7 both within the temple of my mind and out loud, at least a thousand times. The result? On the final day of the test, I was awarded my black belt and the acknowledgment from my longtime mentors in Krav Maga that my performance in the test was at the very top of the class. If you are in need of a positive affirmation and an awesome way to feed your courage wolf, I recommend Psalm 28:7. It worked for me and I believe it can work for you, too.

A WORD OF ENCOURAGEMENT

"Let us encourage one another and build each other up."

—1 Thessalonians 5:11

One of my "extra duty" assignments while serving as a special agent with the Drug Enforcement Administration (DEA) was speaking to fourth- and fifth-grade students about the dangers of drugs, gangs, and crime. I always tried to inspire the kids to realize that with the right mindset and positive-attitude, they could "grow up and be anything they want."

One day, after I had just finished speaking at a low-income school on the outskirts of San Diego County, a young boy walked up to me from the audience, pointed at my shirt—a long-sleeve black shirt with the word "POLICE" in bright yellow printed across the chest—and said, "When I grow up, I want to be a police officer just like you."

I was overjoyed that perhaps my message of positivity and personal belief had gotten through to this boy. I bent over to give the kid a high-five and said, "That's great, you can do it."

To my dismay, the same little boy then shook his head and replied, "No, I can't. My daddy told me I'm going to grow up and be just like him."

For a moment, I hoped that perhaps his dad was a scientist or astronaut or doctor—and that his dad was encouraging him to grow up to be successful, just like he was. With a bit of nervousness in my voice, I asked the boy, "What does your daddy do?"

In a matter-of-fact voice and facial expression, he said, "My daddy is in prison for dealing drugs and he told me I'm going to grow up and be just like him."

In that single moment, time stood still for me and I realized two very important lessons: first, as we go through the course of our day, we never realize if that one little word of encouragement we offer to a friend or loved one—or even a complete stranger—is the first word of encouragement they've received in a day, a week, a month. Or maybe as with that young boy from the outskirts of San Diego—that person's entire life.

Second, at some point in life, the word of encouragement we need to hear the most needs to come from within. When there is nobody to praise us, motivate us, and support us, we still have the power and strength of the Holy Spirit within. We can believe in ourselves. We can encourage each other.

FIVE COACHING TIPS FOR GOAL-SETTING AND POSITIVE SELF-TALK

1. **USE A JOURNAL.** To record your goals and their expected date of achievement. When your goal takes the form of the written word a powerful connection takes place between your head and your heart.

2. **GO PUBLIC.** I encourage the use of public goal-setting. When you communicate your goals to a coach, a friend, or a loved one, a relationship is formed based upon trust and accountability. You become accountable to the other person to give one-hundred percent on the path to accomplishing your goal. In addition, you put a high amount of trust in the other person to keep you accountable to your stated goal.

3. **ENCOURAGE OTHERS.** Ask your friends what they are working towards. If they are uncertain, encourage and teach them how to formulate a goal. Then help them achieve it. Develop a community of *goal-minded* individuals.

4. **SHARE YOUR SUCCESS.** Publicly acknowledge yourself when you achieve a new goal. People want to share in your success and you'll be an inspiration to other people. Let your light shine.

5. **LISTEN VIGILANTLY.** Listen carefully to the words you speak. Your spoken words are a reflection of your true inner self-talk.

As you consider your goals, think big. Goals should provide you with motivation, inspiration, and direction. Goals should fire you up. They should make you jump out of bed in the morning and make you want to devote your free time to them. Learning how to set (and achieve) your goals can radically change your life.

Let's review the three critical points of performance for goal-setting:

1. **The goal must be SPECIFIC.** For example, "I want to complete fifty consecutive gymnastic kipping pull-ups." The more focused the definition, the more opportunity there is for precise planning, preparation, and training. In addition, by specifically defining a goal, an athlete can evaluate with precision when the goal has been met.

2. **Express your goals in the POSITIVE TENSE.** State what you want rather than what you *don't* want. For example, "I want to safely climb to the top of the rope" is said in the positive tense; "I don't want to fall off the rope" is in the negative tense. The key lesson is to keep the mind in a state of positive affirmation of your goal's desired outcome.

3. **The goal must include a TIME FRAME that is challenging yet realistic and achievable.** A goal set too far in the future will lack urgency and fail to create the internal fire needed for accomplishment. On the other hand, too short a time frame can lead to discouragement and despair. In setting a time frame for a goal, weigh the delicate balance between motivating and challenging yourself while simultaneously ensuring a high likelihood of success.

A NOTE ON SUFFERING

The Apostle Paul wrote in his letter to the Church of Philippi that believers in Jesus Christ should, "Rejoice in the Lord always" and not "Be fearful or anxious about anything" (Philippians 4:4-6).

Notice the key word in the Scripture is "always." It wasn't "sometimes" or "on occasion or when it suits you." The expectation was that we "Rejoice in the Lord—always!"

I must confess that I often wish Paul would have said, "Rejoice in the Lord when everything in your life is working out great!" However, through my use of an illustration, take a moment to consider the awesome implications of what Paul is encouraging. The light of God shines equally on all His children. That said, we do not all receive or reflect God's light with the same amount of intensity. Sunlight falls equally on a lump of coal and a diamond but only the diamond receives and reflects the light with beauty and splendor. The carbon in the coal has the potential to become a diamond. All that the coal requires is a season of suffering, immense pressure, and intense testing. In other words, the conversion from coal to diamond necessitates the coal becoming comfortable with the uncomfortable.

Paul knew that suffering would lead the believer to experience a conversion of their soul into the likeness of Jesus Christ. And for this reason, I believe that we can join Paul and "Shout for joy over our victory and lift up our hands in the name of God" (Psalm 20:5) during every season of challenge and suffering that we face.

— SEVEN AFFIRMATIONS FOR A POSITIVE MINDSET —

In addition to repeating Bible verse, I have developed seven super powerful affirmations for you to repeat each morning:

1. *"I believe in myself and I love myself and I constantly reaffirm my ability to succeed."* (I created this affirmation for Ultimate Fighting Championship [UFC] legend Gray Maynard; Brazilian Jiu-jitsu Black Belt world champion Nathan Mendelsohn; and six-time multi-division world champion professional boxer Robert "The Ghost" Guerrero.)

2. *"I am whole, strong, powerful, loving, harmonious, and happy."*

3. *"God is entirely devoted to my personal advancement."* (Special recognition to my late mother, Julianne, who taught me this affirmation!)

4. *"Each day of my life, I increase in wisdom, stature, and strength."* (Based on Luke 2:52.)

5. *"I can overcome any challenge set before me."* (Based on Philippians 4:13.)

6. *"I am a brave man (or woman) and strong. I am a warrior and God is with me."* (Based on 1 Samuel 16:18.)

7. *"God is my strength, and my shield; my heart trusts in Him and He helps me"* (Psalm 28:7).

That seventh one is my favorite lately.

Up until now, we have discovered the importance of self mastery, breathing, meditation, and the power of positive self-talk. To reinforce how important these concepts are, I want to now return to the mystical world of *The Warrior and The Monk* to reiterate these principles in a fable. In the words of Wise Monk:

"Remember this sequence of events, and you can assure yourself a future of prosperity, love, and fulfillment:

Positive Thoughts lead to Positive Words, which produce after their kind, resulting in positive experiences within every area of your life."

The young warrior then asked the wise monk,

"How can I influence the quality of my thinking?"

"This question, young warrior..."

replied the wise monk,

"Is a very good question, indeed."

The wise monk then continued,

"A warrior must be skillful both in action, and non-action.[6]

Action is the world of effects, and non-action is the world of cause. The first step, therefore, is to remove yourself from the world of effects, and to become still."

The young warrior asked,

"Do you mean, I just have to sit down, and stop moving?"

The wise monk laughed and replied,

"Yes! The first step is as simple as that. When the body becomes still, the mind will surely follow. I also recommend closing your eyes, which will help turn your attention inward. When you focus your attention inward, you are able to connect with God." [7]

◆◆◆

The wise monk then continued to increase the wisdom and knowledge of the young warrior.

"The next step is to become aware of your breathing. The quality of your breathing, the quality of your posture, and the quality of your thinking, are all intimately connected. Bringing your awareness to your breathing, your posture, and your thinking is known as 'mindfulness,' which means to hold your awareness on the present moment and task at hand."

The young warrior asked, "How can I develop awareness of my breath?"

"When you breathe in, know that you are breathing in," answered the wise monk, "And when you breathe out, know that you are breathing out."

Perplexed by this seemingly obvious instruction, the young warrior defensively replied,

"I have been breathing just fine my entire life."

Full of patience, the wise monk explained,

"Automatic breathing and mindful breathing are worlds apart. In the moments that you are intensely aware of the inhalation and exhalation within a single breathing cycle, you become fully alive in the present moment. Although your mind can regress to the past, or project into the future, your breath is always right here, right now — like an anchor for your soul." [8]

◆◆◆◆

Due to the young warrior's extensive training within the world of action, he was well aware of the significance of respiratory conditioning. The young warrior reflected on moments in his life when his ability to command his breathing while overcoming dragons was absolutely critical to victory.

Full of promise and intrigue, the young warrior exclaimed,

"The power of the breath is something I feel compelled to learn more about. In addition to bringing awareness to every inhalation and exhalation, what else do you recommend I do?"

The wise monk continued to elaborate on the significance of the breath...

"The inhalation should be long, slow, subtle, deep, and should evenly spread throughout the entire body. Each in-breath draws energy from the atmosphere into the cells of the lungs. This rejuvenates the spiritual force within you. By briefly holding the breath once drawn in, the energy is fully absorbed. This evenly distributes it through all the systems of your body.

The slow and peaceful exhalation removes mental and physical toxins that have been accumulated. Pause briefly after the out-breath so that all mental stress is purged away. The mind is then naturally drawn into the presence of God."

With a look of awe and wonder on his face, the young warrior remarked,

"I had no idea so much transformation could take place within a single breath!"

Smiling broadly, the wise monk said,

"Indeed, young warrior, a daily breath practice can enhance every aspect of your life. This is why the ancient Prophets said, 'The breath of God gives life.'" [9]

The young warrior inquired,

"What constitutes a breath practice?"

The wise monk answered,

"Even one conscious breath a day is sufficient to experience all the benefits of a breath practice." [10]

The wise monk then proposed they sit together and experience the power of physical stillness, upright posture, and mindful breathing.

Directing the young warrior to sit with his body, neck, and head held firmly in a straight line with his eyes closed, the wise monk then led him through an ancient breathing practice designed to bring the mind to a state of restful alertness. [11]

The wise monk began by saying...

"Be sure to **breathe through your nose** the entire time.

Now **inhale** and count to four....

Retain the breath for another four count....

Exhale for a four count....

Suspend the breath for a four count." [12]

The wise monk and the young warrior continued this breathing sequence for a total of four rounds.

As the breathing practice concluded, a large smile appeared on the young warrior's face.

"I feel wonderful!" exclaimed the young warrior.

"I always knew the benefit of upright posture. However, I never realized something as simple as physical stillness and mindful breathing could have such a profound effect on me."

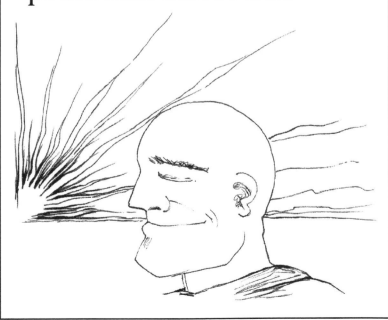

FIRST WORDS

The very first words you speak each day are vital and will have a profound impact on the quality of your life experience. When you wake up, your mind is like the flat surface of a pond. You want to toss the right stone into the center of that pond so that the ripples that flow from it help you set the right energy and direction for the day. The stone and rippling effect are a metaphor for the power of your first spoken words. They ripple across the entire ocean of the universe.

"A warrior must be skillfull in both movement and stillness."
—MARK DIVINE

Here is how I approach my "First Words" each morning. Upon waking, I allow myself to embrace the stillness and silence of the moment. Without speaking, I move quietly to the kitchen and pour a glass of water. As I drink, I allow a feeling of gratitude for the water.

I then shift to an awareness of my breathing and might perform alternate nostril breathing. I then move to a place to sit and conduct a simple and brief seated meditation, my mind aware of the inward and outward flow of breath. From this stillness, I allow the words to form in my mind that will be my first spoken words of the day. These words are chosen carefully, breaking the morning silence in a self-affirming way.

When I teach yoga, I say the following: "I encourage you now to practice the warrior tradition of First Words. The practice is such that when you speak, you imagine your spoken word rippling through the fertile soil of the universe, ultimately manifesting and touching every corner of your life. Therefore, speak your First Words with light, love, and positive expectancy."

Keep in mind that every time you speak, you are speaking into silence. Therefore, First Words are most powerful in the morning because of the length of time you have been in silence. However, even in the middle of a heated conversation, you can take a breath, internally pause, and then practice First Words.

Personally, I always break the sacred silence of the early morning hours with a Bible verse. However, your First Words can be inspired from within the wisdom of your soul. Just ensure your they are always offered with "light, love, and positive expectancy."

A WARRIOR TRADITION STORY ON LOVING KINDNESS

Many years ago, the Sun and the Wind decided to hold a competition to determine who was the strongest. Gazing down onto the earth, Sun and Wind spotted an old man walking along a worn path.

"See the old man walking alone on the path? Whoever can get the old man to remove his winter coat is surely the strongest between us," Wind remarked to Sun.

"Very well," said Sun, "You may display your strength first."

The Sun silently departed and hid behind a cloud. The Wind began to howl and scream and cause great torment. However, the harder the Wind blew, the more determined the old man was to keep his winter coat pulled tightly against his body. Finally, the Wind gave up and summoned the Sun.

Returning from behind the cloud, the Sun began to shine brightly onto the old man. The clouds departed, the sky turned bright blue, and warmth filled the air.

"My goodness," remarked the old man, "What a beautiful day it has become. It is far too hot for this winter coat."

With these words, the old man removed his coat and continued to walk along the path.

In my experience on the warrior's path, I've found we can accomplish far more, with less effort, when we call upon our innate power to be kind and loving. This can be quite a shift from the normally conditioned patterns of thought: we react harshly to people and circumstances that disrupt our peace of mind. However, the mark of a disciplined warrior is to remain non-reactive to external events. A true warrior knows the external world is a perfect reflection of their internal world. By practicing loving kindness to ourselves, we maintain the power over our thoughts and actions and forge the ability to remain an anchor in the storms of life.

— *LEADERSHIP IN THE WARRIOR TRADITION* —

One of the incredible benefits of developing your mind, body, and spirit is the natural tendency for you to increase your capacity as a world-class leader. I learned something important on the subject from one of my dear friends, Jason Redman, a former Navy SEAL and author of the bestselling book, *The Trident – The Forging and Reforging of a Navy SEAL Leader.* Jason once told me, "In order to effectively lead other people, you have to first lead yourself."

Mark Divine and I shared a similar concept during a podcast we were co-featured on when we defined leadership as "self-mastery in the service of others." As you engage in the *Victory* integrated program, you are mastering yourself. The degree of self-mastery you achieve will support your intention to lead others. Let me give you an illustration of what leadership means to me.

IN THE PRESENCE OF A LEADER

In December 2004, Coach Glassman, Josh Everett, Kurtis Bowler, and I traveled to Fort Lewis, Washington, to conduct a private three-day CrossFit seminar for members of the Army 1st Special Forces Group.

In the early days of the CrossFit training program, we placed a huge emphasis on what we termed "performance on demand," as attendees and instructors were called to perform upwards of three grueling CrossFit workouts a day.

This seminar was very exciting for me. I had recently returned from Army Basic Combat Training and was two weeks away from beginning

Officer Candidate School. I was honored to be in the presence of established leaders and warriors so I could apply the skills they would undoubtedly teach me to my upcoming training. Little did I know that one particular display of leadership would leave a lasting impression on me for the rest of my life.

Mark Divine has been a great example of a warrior leader in my life.

As the sun begin to set on Sunday evening and the course drew to a close, Coach briefed the instructors and soldiers on the final workout. Josh and I had participated in each of the five workouts. Because this was a military certification, Coach had upped the volume and duration of the classic CrossFit events. As a result, we had completed five rounds of Helen (run four hundred meters, twenty-one kettlebell swings, twelve pull-ups) and what we called "big fat" versions of Fran and Elizabeth—twenty-one, eighteen, fifteen, twelve, nine, six, and then three reps of the thruster/pull-up and barbell clean/ring-dip couplets. Needless to say, there was not a lot of enthusiasm for the final workout of the day.

As we gathered around Coach, I noticed all the instructors and soldiers looked extremely exhausted. We were dirty, sweaty, and hungry. We had our hands on our knees to keep from falling over and I had a hard time concentrating on the instructions for the workout. Because I was about to embark upon an intense military leadership course, I had been paying close attention to the senior officer of the group. I wanted to see firsthand what true leaders said and did to inspire and motivate those people in their command.

The officer in charge that weekend was Capt. Perry., an extremely athletic individual. He was physically capable of setting an example for his men to follow. He eagerly participated in all the workouts during the weekend and consistently achieved some of the fastest times and highest scores in the events. Although he was very confident, I observed that he was also very humble, always putting the welfare of both the CrossFit instructors and his soldiers before himself.

As we huddled together to receive Coach's instructions, I was eager to see how Capt. Perry would raise the spirits of his soldiers to attack the final workout.

When Coach finished the brief, he turned to the captain and said, "Sir, go ahead and choose five of your men to complete this workout." Capt. Perry looked into the eyes of his soldiers and took note of their physical and mental state. Realizing that his soldiers, as well as Josh and I, were well beyond our ability to perform athletically, Capt. Perry did what he did best: he led by example and from the front. He took a deep breath and rolled his shoulders back. In a firm voice filled with utter resolve he said, "It's okay, men. I've got this one."

With that, he charged forward into the workout. The second he said those words and took his first step, there was an immediate change in the mental and physical composure of the group. A collective surge of energy filled the air and we all enthusiastically charged after the captain.

By his words and actions, Capt. Perry instilled in me what might be one of the most important leadership lessons there is: *a leader must lead by example and from the front.*

I embraced the lesson he taught me that day and did my best to set a positive example in everything I did from that moment on. Whether it be in CrossFit, law enforcement, or any endeavor of my life, I always strive to lead like Capt. Perry and encourage you to do the same.

MENTAL ATTRIBUTES OF WARRIOR LEADERSHIP

In addition to gaining *physical* capacity in the following ten skills, have the assurance that you will also be developing their *mental* equivalent, which will greatly enhance your ability as a leader.[13]

Endurance: The ability to maintain belief in self and others.

Stamina: The ability to create and maintain intense mental effort, focus, and resilience.

Strength: The ability to maintain resolve of decision.

Flexibility: (1) The ability to independently choose an emotional reaction to a wide range of external circumstances. (2) The ability to apply versatile methods to the accomplishment of a fixed goal.

Power: (1) The ability to encourage self and others in the pursuit of a worthy goal. (2) The ability to immediately generate an intense state of motivation and positive expectancy.

Speed: The ability to make immediate command decisions in the face of opposition, challenge, and uncertainty.

Coordination: The ability to invoke the most productive emotional response at a given time and place.

Agility: (1) The ability to support the needs of others while ensuring personal goals and challenges are fulfilled. (2) The ability to respond to environment and circumstance with deliberate attitudes and beliefs so as to achieve a desired end state.

Balance: (1) The ability to maintain individual physical, mental, and spiritual wellness. (2) The ability to maintain a positive state of mind or attitude regardless of external stimuli.

Accuracy: (1) The ability to set and achieve specific and concise goals. (2) The ability to listen and correctly identify internal thoughts, emotions, and energies.

MENTAL NUTRITION

In December 2003, in lieu of a traditional CrossFit WOD (a CrossFit term for 'Workout Of the Day'), Coach gathered the 6 a.m. "Team Six" athletes around the whiteboard for a lecture on the theoretical development in the hierarchy of an athlete. This lecture, like most of the conversations, seminars, and interactions I had with the coach, proved to be life-changing.

Coach explained that if he intended to forge the ultimate athlete, he would start with nutrition. He believed that nutrition was so important in the development and sustainment of an athlete, that in a perfect world, he would put an athlete on an island for thirty days with nothing to do except eat the right way. During a previous lecture from Coach in February 2002, I had learned that by "eat the right way," he was referring to a balance of 40-percent carbohydrate, 30-percent protein, and 30-percent fat, which would yield a balanced hormonal response in the athlete and ultimately result in leaner muscle mass and increased athletic capacity in the gym.

1 / 23 RULE

Coach provided several compelling reasons for the focus on nutrition, the first was a simple rule he called the "1 to 23 Rule." He explained that most athletes train in CrossFit approximately one hour a day. This left twenty-three additional hours during the day in which the athlete would have to make a choice: would he or she use the time outside the gym to support or unravel the hour that had been invested while inside the gym?

Coach proposed that the best way to support the invested hour was with nutrition. After all, with the recommendation of the Zone Diet, most athletes would eat between four and six times during the day.

This simple ratio of time spent training to time spent eating was compelling enough for me to realize that making conscious choices about my food intake was absolutely essential in my development as an athlete.

$$\frac{1}{23}$$

What will you do with the other 23 hours outside the gym?

THE GLASS CEILING RULE

The second example Coach used, he referred to as the "Glass Ceiling Rule." In this example, he used my personal experience and the experiences of the other athletes from Team Six to make his point. He drew seven circles in a row on the whiteboard and explained that each circle represented one of the athletes of Team Six. He reminded us of our accomplishments and our ultimate plateau in the gym only one year before. Indeed, each of the athletes had seemed to reach an invisible ceiling and our performances in the gym had all tapered off. We were finishing the WODs within a few seconds of each other, with no athlete ever achieving complete dominance over the workouts.

Coach had recommended the implementation of the Zone Diet and I had been the first athlete to use the diet for two weeks with complete accuracy and discipline. On the whiteboard, he drew an arrow from the circle that represented me straight up so that my circle was now approximately six inches above the other athletes. He explained that given the fact that all other variables were constant, my increased athletic performance had been a direct result of my change in nutrition. He was indeed correct. In just two weeks, I had noticeably increased my athletic performance, body proportions, and mental clarity relative to the other athletes who had not yet started the diet.

Coach then drew another arrow from one of the remaining six circles straight up, now even with my circle. He explained that this circle represented Brazilian jiu-jitsu world champion Mike Weaver, also a loyal member of Team Six. After witnessing my improvement, Mike had been the next athlete to use the diet—with similar astounding results.

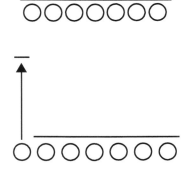

*The Glass-Ceiling Rule: If all athletes are equal (top),
improving the diet will give one a huge boost in performance.*

Finally, Coach drew arrows above all the remaining circles, explaining that as each of the Team Six athletes started to eat the right way, their capacity in the gym dramatically improved.

After thoroughly convincing us of the importance of nutrition as the foundation in the development of an athlete, Coach moved on to the next building block: *metabolic conditioning*. After an athlete had the right fuel in the body, it was time to start to burn the fuel and get the body systems moving. Metabolic conditioning referred to modalities such as running, cycling, swimming, and rowing.

Next in the development of an athlete came *gymnastics,* and this is where Coach's eyes really lit up. He had a deep love and respect for gymnastics and his definition was broad and inclusive. By "gymnastics movements," he included any skill that used the body's own weight as a means of resistance. Pull-ups, push-ups, rope-climbing, handstands, squats (body weight and single-leg), dips, and L-sits were among some of his favorite physical examples of these skills.

Coach was adamant that athletes even remotely interested in achieving elite fitness should begin with a solid foundation of being in control of their body in space and time.

Next in the theoretical development of an athlete came *weightlifting.* The next logical progression once body control was achieved was control over an external object. By weightlifting, he referred to compound, multi-joint movements that did one thing: moved a large load a long distance quickly.

Again, Coach's voice picked up in excitement and passion as he explained with a mathematical equation the potential for movements—such as a snatch, clean and jerk, and deadlift—to create power that was rivaled only by an animal: a horse!

He used me as an example to demonstrate the potential I had to produce power during a workout such as Fran. By measuring the distance my center of mass (my belly button) traveled during the thruster and pull-up (nearly four feet per repetition), as well as the distance the ninety-five-pound barbell traveled per repetition (nearly six feet), Coach demonstrated that in approximately three minutes of work, I would produce and sustain nearly two-thirds of one horsepower.

The significance of this power output was that it equated with CrossFit's definition of "intensity." Intensity being "*the independent variable most commonly associated with maximizing the rate of return on favorable adaptation to exercise.*" (That was a direct quote from Coach I had written in my journal during his lecture that day.)

Finally, after an athlete had built a solid foundation in nutrition, metabolic conditioning, gymnastics, and weightlifting, it was time to have some fun and express our newfound capacity in *sport*. Keep in mind, these were the days before the formal development of the CrossFit Games.

Coach's belief was that fitness should be expressed by constantly learning and playing new sports. As with other terms, his view of sport was extremely broad. He encouraged his athletes to rock climb, scuba dive, surf, bicycle race, train in martial arts and, of course, continue to achieve more work in less time during the classic CrossFit WODs.

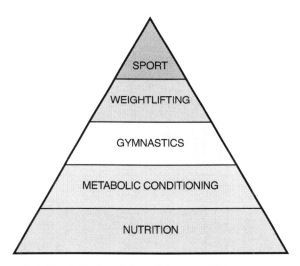

Nutrition is the foundation of the pyramid for a reason.

Coach then warned us that at if at any time our capacity in sport (the WOD or a sporting event outside the gym) should start to suffer or see retrograde performance, we should immediately return to the foundation and refocus our attention on nutrition. Indeed, nutrition was a direct representation of an athlete's potential for elite performance in *any* physical endeavor.

I sat on a medicine ball that day in front of Coach and the whiteboard, taking pages of notes in my fitness journal. I was captivated by the notion that nutrition would play such a significant role in my development as an athlete. What was most exciting about the prospect of his lecture was that I retained complete control and influence over what I ate during the day. The choice was entirely mine; all it took was conscious decision-making every time I sat down to eat.

THE AMAZING PARADIGM SHIFT

A little less than three months after listening to Coach's lecture on the theoretical development of an athlete, I found myself on a Greyhound bus on my way to Fort Sill, Oklahoma, for Army Basic Combat Training. After working as a deputy sheriff for several years, I felt compelled to serve concurrently in the Army and had decided to enlist in the Army National Guard.

As I sat quietly, several thoughts went through my mind, the loudest and most constant being, "What in the world am I doing in Oklahoma?" I was twenty-four years old when I went through boot camp, which, at the time was considered "old" for initial training and enlistment. On the bus with me on that lonesome drive were seventeen- and eighteen-year-olds, some between their junior and senior years of high school, some having just graduated.

I knew the power of staying positive in thought and word from previous life experiences with CrossFit and my experience as a deputy sheriff but the other future soldiers apparently did not. On the bus that day, I heard a neverending stream of statements that revolved around fear, anger, depression, and anxiety.

Finally, we rolled to a stop inside the gates of Fort Sill. A sea of drill sergeants immediately surrounded the bus and began taunting us with menacing faces and gestures. Two fierce-looking drill sergeants stormed aboard and screamed, "Get off my bus right now and line up on the yellow lines!"

I stumbled off the bus and quickly stood at attention on the yellow lines painted on the cement in front of the barracks. The yellow lines served a purpose, allowing new recruits with no military experience to quickly assemble into a formation. Suddenly, my senior drill instructor walked in front of the formation and called the group to attention.

I will always remember him and the first few words of wisdom he shared with me and the other future soldiers on that day: "Listen up, *prives*!" said Staff Sgt. Oliver. He would not refer to us as "privates" for nine more weeks, when we graduated boot camp. "Boot camp will be hard enough physically, so don't beat yourself up mentally."

Hearing these words, I leaned in and paid close attention. His advice seemed familiar, almost like something Coach would say. "In my Army, I want warriors, and warriors think a certain way," Sgt. Oliver said. "In boot camp, your thoughts will become your words, your words will become your actions, your actions will become your habits, your habits will become your character, and your character will determine your destiny. And I want warriors!"

The staff sergeant's words resonated with me. I knew he was right: to be successful at boot camp, I had to remain positive in both thought and word.

That night as I lay in my bunk bed, I could not sleep. I thought about my friends at CrossFit Santa Cruz and all the catching up I would have to do when I got back. I pulled the wool blanket over my head and turned on my little red-lens flashlight so I would not disturb the guys sleeping next to me. I took out my CrossFit training journal from Santa Cruz and looked back over a few months of training data and notes.

Suddenly, I came across the lecture and diagram from February in which Coach had drawn the triangle on the white board that explained the theoretical development of an athlete. In an instant, I was wide awake with excitement with one of those compelling light-bulb moments. Looking at the diagram, I drew another diagram next to it. At the bottom, to represent nutrition, I wrote "thoughts and words." At the top of the diagram, to represent sport, I wrote "destiny."

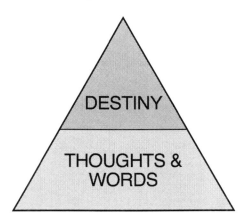

I realized that in the same way that *physical* nutrition (the foods we eat) represents the foundation of our athletic capacity, *mental* nutrition (our thoughts and words) represents the foundation of our development as we strive to achieve our greatest self, both inside and outside the gym.

THINKING THE RIGHT WAY

The Zone Diet, which Dr. Barry Sears introduced in 1995, is his term for proper hormone balance. He says that a 40-30-30 caloric balance of low-glycemic carbs (mostly fruits and vegetables), low-fat protein, and fat has several great effects on the body. These include the release of moderate amounts of the hormones insulin and glycogen, resulting in the release of a flood of feel-good chemicals called eicosanoids, which do a bunch of good things: protect the heart, open the bronchi of the lungs, and reduce inflammation. A secondary effect of importance to CrossFit athletes is noticeable fat loss and increased physical capacity.

The important consideration often overlooked in the Zone Diet (or any diet, for that matter) is *choice*. Every time we put food or beverage into our mouth, we are faced with a choice: will our physical nutrition support or unravel our investment of time in the gym? The best food choices in the world are good for us only in theory until the moment they are consumed. It is the conscious act of choosing and consuming the right physical nutrition that ultimately makes a positive difference in our lives.

Like most of the lessons of the CrossFit gym, I strive to draw a correlate between what is true inside the gym and what is true outside the gym. I realized with Sgt. Oliver's mentorship that our thoughts and words are the nutrition of our lives and ultimately determine who we become and what we are capable of achieving.

Just as with physical nutrition, which consists of three broad types of food (protein, carbohydrate, and fat), mental nutrition offers three broad types of thinking and speaking: **empowering words**, **mantras**, and **affirmations**.

EMPOWERING WORDS: CHOOSING THE RIGHT MENTAL NUTRITION

When we prepare a meal, we have a choice about the types of carbohydrate we consume. Although both cookies and apples are considered carbohydrate, we understand the benefit of choosing the apple instead of the cookie. Individual food choice is important and we benefit from increased health and wellness when we choose the right foods. In the same manner, we have an opportunity to choose empowering words to consume, as well.

Refer to the list below:
- "Hard" vs. "Challenging"
- "Injury" vs. "Resilience"
- "Lazy" vs. "Determined"
- "Weak" vs. "Strong"
- "Sick" vs. "Healthy"

Some of the most empowering words available for athletes to "consume" are the ten words associated with the general physical skills we train for in the gym. Although normally associated with physical fitness, each word also holds an important definition related to character development and the person we become outside the gym. (See mental attributes of warrior leadership, page 63.)

MANTRAS: DEVELOPING HEALTHY DAYTIME SNACKS

Once we have begun to consume the right food, it's time to start designing healthy bite-size snacks. A mantra is *a concise conscious thought pattern or verbalized statement about something we want to express in the moment*. One simple way to achieve this is to add the words such as "I am" or "I have" before the ten general physical skills.

The beauty of this exercise is that we are able to use a brief mantra to solicit a response both physically and mentally in the body. For example, "I am flexible" or "I have endurance." The one important consideration and rule for developing mantras is to stay in the positive tense. By positive tense, I simply mean to state in the mantra what you want as opposed to what you lack or don't want. Again, the subconscious mind doesn't hear words of negation.

For example, "Don't fall" vs. "Hold tightly," or "Don't trip" vs. "Retain agility." One of the best examples of how easy it is to slip into the negative tense came during a CrossFit goal-setting course in Colorado. One of the athletes in attendance had written on his red *Inov8* shoes what he had originally thought was a good mantra. On the left shoe he had written, "Don't" and on the right "Stop."

The intent was that during a workout or a long-distance run, he would look down at the mantra on his shoes for inspiration and would see "Don't Stop."

We discussed a more powerful word choice and mantra: "Keep going." With a laugh, he quickly lined through the old mantra and wrote in big bold letters, "Keep going!"

AFFIRMATIONS: BUILDING COMPLETE MEALS

Once we are consuming the right foods and eating healthy snacks, it's time to begin building complete meals. I refer to the complete meal as an affirmation. Affirmations are *statements verbalized in the present tense about positive outcomes we want to achieve in the future.*

For example:
- *"I believe in myself and my ability to succeed."*
- *"I am a natural athlete and quickly learn new skills."*
- *"I always give my best effort during a workout and leave it all on the gym floor."*
- *"I encourage myself and others by setting a positive example."*

PART TWO
THE SPIRIT

PART TWO: THE SPIRIT

As I pointed out before, my life was forever changed by Coach Glassman's pearl of wisdom that, "The greatest adaptation to CrossFit takes place between the ears." That principle is consistent with the words of the Bible. When the prophet Samuel was directed by God to locate and anoint the next king of Israel, the Lord warned him not to be concerned with outward appearances. "The LORD does not look at the things people look at. People look at the outward appearance but the LORD looks at the heart" (1 Samuel 16:7).

I believe this verse from Scripture is one of the most compelling reasons why anyone participating in a physical fitness program (*outward appearances*) must also develop a spiritual practice (*inward spiritual growth and maturity*) in order to achieve their full potential.

Therefore, the question before us is this: "What is a spiritual practice?"

Dr. Kelly Starrett is a dear friend, mentor, bestselling author, and the creator of the MobilityWOD website, where he offers up an encyclopedia's worth of education and problem-solving on improving positions, movement, and power output. He has a global following and consults with NFL teams, top MLB players, Tour de France cyclists, and special operations components from both military and law enforcement. During speaking engagements, he often poses a question to the audience: "Do you have a movement practice?"

For Kelly, having a movement practice such as yoga or Pilates means dedicating a block of time to working toward improving your mobility and ability to assume and hold good positions. You might have your sport—cycling, rowing, basketball, CrossFit, surfing—and that's great but to support your sport and your life in general, he advises people to build a movement practice.

Kelly's question—the motivation behind it and the importance he places upon it—makes a helpful entryway into our discussion of the spiritual dimension of *Victory*. In the same way he suggests finding a movement practice as a form of support, I am advocating that you develop specific spiritual practices with the goal of developing your "true core."

The concept of the *core* in athletics, and CrossFit in particular, is well known. The principle involves utilizing the midsection, hips, and large erector muscles of the low back to create a wave of lateral contraction throughout the body. In the context of weightlifting or controlling any external object, the athlete is always strongest when keeping the external object closest to the core. However, when focusing on the spiritual dimension of our growth, we have to move beyond the *physical* core to the *spiritual* core of our being.

I am extremely passionate about teaching spiritual principles within the framework of storytelling, specifically, the use of parables and fables. Undoubtedly, my love for storytelling and respect for the power of parables comes from my study of God's Word, and the manner in which Jesus Christ taught his disciples.

I am not here to advocate a particular religion. However, I would be amiss if I did not confess that I attribute any and all identifiable success I have achieved in life to my faith in God, and the redeeming work of His Son Jesus Christ. Furthermore, I have discovered that the single biggest variable that positively affects growth in all dimensions of my body, mind, and spirit, is the Word of God as revealed within the Holy Bible.

Consider the words of the Apostle Paul to really drive this point home: "All Scripture [the Holy Bible] is God-breathed [inspired by God] and is useful for teaching, rebuking, correcting, and training in righteousness [right thinking, leading to right speaking, thus, resulting in right action], so that you may be thoroughly equipped for every good work" (2 Timothy 3:16-17).[14]

Ponder for a moment the remarkable benefits of even a rudimentary understanding of Scripture. Consider the Bible verse which says, "As iron sharpens iron, so one person sharpens another" (Proverbs 27:17). This is an awesome verse that carries resounding implications within the warrior tradition. However, in addition to being sharpened and held accountable by another person, it is also important to remember that Scripture teaches that God is our *ultimate* source of strength, tempering, forging, and sharpening (refer to the story on page 41).

God designed you in His image, and therefore, the Spirit dwelling within you is a source of "power, love, and self-discipline" (2 Timothy 1:7), which can be your greatest source of strength throughout the various challenges and seasons of your life.

I'm a Christian, so that is an important part of my personal spiritual practice. That is what's right for me. However, as renowned yoga teacher Rolf Gates once told me, "All spiritual paths ultimately lead to the same light." Christianity, a conservative Baptist theology, and the spiritual disciplines that I teach in this book have been the right path for me but it might not be right for you. Find the spiritual path that speaks to your heart and moral compass, then dedicate yourself to that pursuit.

Whatever path you choose, ensure that you are guided by the Word of God as revealed within the Bible. Without it to guide your path, it can become easy to fall into the trap of trusting worldly wisdom or, worse yet, trusting yourself. Knowing the danger of relying solely on ourselves or the wisdom of the world, the Bible teaches that we should instead, "Trust in the LORD with all your heart and lean not on your own understanding. In all your ways submit to God, and he will make your paths straight" (Proverbs 3:5-6).

In my experience, there is no achieving optimal physical performance in the gym—or happiness, meaning, purpose, fulfillment in life—without developing a spiritual practice. Furthermore, in order to really express your unique God-given talents and abilities, and achieve your "mission in life," a dedicated spiritual practice is absolutely vital.

My dear friend Londale Theus, a former SWAT officer and one of the best Krav Maga martial art instructors in the world, echoes this sentiment when he talks about the power of a spiritual practice: "It's impossible to achieve your potential unless you develop a spiritual practice as a part of your life. It just won't happen."

When physical training gets extremely uncomfortable, how do you keep going? When you're in the middle of an especially tough workout and a negative voice in your head suggests it's time to quit, where do you dig? During any challenging circumstance when everything seems stacked against you, how do you maintain personal belief and keep marching forward? Outside the gym, how do you respond to the challenges that life presents to you? When there's loss and hardship and tragedy, and those supreme difficulties that are part of being human become your testing ground, how do you maintain your life path, intentions, and goals?

Often, the strength we need to cultivate and rely on most lies in the spiritual realm.

As I will elaborate on in the following section, it is important to note the key difference between a physical practice and a spiritual practice has to do with the intended purpose of the practice. In other words, the intention of a physical practice is to develop physical attributes, increase in physical strength, and achieve peak physical wellness and fitness in the body. Although there are certainly intangible mental benefits to a physical practice (after all, Coach did say the greatest adaptation to a physical practice would, in fact, be mental), the intention remains an overt focus on the body.

On the other hand, the intention of a spiritual practice is to "increase in wisdom, stature, and favor with God and mankind" (Luke 2:52) and to "discipline ourselves for the purpose of godliness" (1 Timothy 4:7).

In addition to teaching you a series of spiritual disciplines that you can use in developing a spiritual practice, I also want to introduce a key spiritual principle that is absolutely essential in achieving breakthroughs, success, and favor within every area of your life: this is the spiritual practice of *forgiveness*.

However, before we discuss the spiritual disciplines, I want to make sure your eyes are open — the eyes of your heart, that is.

THE EYES OF OUR HEART

Throughout the Bible, it becomes apparent that seeing clearly requires more than physical eyes. As the Psalmist writes, "Open the eyes of our heart, O God, so that we can see" (Psalm 119:18). What I want to share with you is something radical. Scripture teaches us how to expand our vision by opening a faculty of our being that is far more important than our sense of sight.

The Old Testament tells a story about the Prophet Elisha that is at the heart of this deeper source of seeing. The fact that it's embedded in a story is, I've learned, quite significant. When I was starting in law enforcement in 2001, one of my mentors said to me, "Greg, if you tell me the truth, I will believe you. If you tell me a fact, I will listen. However, if you share with me a story, I will *remember*." (What's so incredible about studying the Word of God is that it contains all three—truths, facts, and stories—at the same time; we learn about the Word of God through story, yet these stories contain truths and facts that are applicable to us as much today as any other time in history.)

A rival king named Aram had been unsuccessfully attempting to overthrow the king of Israel but every time he planned an attack, God would provide Elisha with details of it—the time, place, size of the enemy army, etc.—and the prophet would warn Israel's king, who would then act accordingly, thwarting the assault.

King Aram got wise to Elisha's inside information and decided that rather than attack the king, he ought to assassinate the prophet. So, early one morning, his army—featuring an intimidating force of a then-state-of-the-art military unit, the chariot—surrounded the city. Elisha's servant observed the siege and reported back, saying, "Oh no, what shall we do?"

Elisha replied with one of my favorite lines from Scripture, "Do not be afraid, the forces that are for us are greater than the forces that are against us" (2 Kings 6:16). Then, he prayed for his servant, "Open his eyes, Lord, so that he may see" (2 Kings 6:17).

God did so. The servant looked again and saw that between him and the enemy there was another army of chariots, which were afire (representing God's presence). Indeed, their forces really were greater than King Aram's.

Let's break this story down and distill the revelation, wisdom, and knowledge God is intending to share. Elisha and his servant were asleep. During the night, King Aram dispatched his chariot-led army to lay siege to the city. This isn't your run-of-the-mill infantry, armed with primitive cudgels, unsophisticated projectiles, iron or—best-case scenario—bronze short swords. No, these are elite troops. And during the night, they've positioned themselves stealthily around the city.

When the servant wakes up, he goes outside, sees the enemy forces, and freaks out. He goes back to Elisha and asks what they should do. Elisha surveys the scene and sees something entirely different. So, he says, "Do not be afraid, the forces that are for us are greater than the forces that are against us."

Clearly, both men were looking at the same thing but saw vastly different realities. That's when Elisha realized, "This guy isn't seeing what's really there," prompting him to pray that God would "open his eyes," so that they could see the same thing.

When God did just that, the servant saw that the city was protected by an even larger regiment of fiery chariots.

Immediately, it's obvious that this story is attempting to relate something at the metaphysical level as opposed to merely the physical level because the servant's eyes were just as open as Elisha's (and probably much wider given his panicked reaction). Let's be clear, Scripture doesn't say the servant heard the chariots' horses or sensed their presence—it says he saw them with his own eyes. Thus, those must not have been the eyes that God opened per Elisha's prayer. God opened the "eyes" of his heart, enabling him to see in a deeper sense.

This seems to suggest that we do not see things as *they* are; we see things as *we* are. That implies that at any time, we have the capacity to change the way we look at something. And, as has been pointed out in the section on mindset, when we change the way we look at something, that which we look at begins to change.

From this passage of Scripture, I draw three essential truths that God is revealing.

First, and as I've pointed out in Part I, whatever we focus our attention on becomes magnified in our lives. Similarly, if we remove our attention from something, it will dissolve and fade away. This being the case, we can learn to control our focus by developing the necessary willpower. Rather than being passive spectators to our focus, we can control where the magnifying glass is aimed.

Second is that our thinking influences the quality of what we see. That truth is revealed to us through this Scripture. Remember, the servant's eyes were *already* open. So, why did Elisha pray that God would "open his eyes?" We must not be talking about eyeballs in this case. So, God opened the "eyes" of his heart. If that anthropomorphic language seems a bit larger than life, remember that in the millennia before Freud, no one had developed the concept of a subconscious, much less a terminology. For readers of the Bible, it would be imperative to explain such concepts in a tangible vernacular.

Interestingly, the word the biblical author arrived on—"heart"—has much more meaningfulness in its connotation than our sterilized "subconscious." Consider the heart's function: circulation of the life's blood. By asking God to open the eyes of the heart, we're asking for a change of circulation. Thus, a "change of heart" is a life-altering prayer, whereas "changing one's mind" is just whimsical.

Third, and perhaps most important, we are able to improve the quality of our thinking. How? By allowing the intellect to rest in the presence of God. He, in fact, wants to reveal to us the reality of that which we see. God wanted the servant to see as Elisha saw.

This means that despite what forces may seem to be arrayed against us, it isn't necessarily the case that they outnumber the forces that are with us. God wants us to see the reality of the battlefield.

Now, let's take these three truths and apply the authority of Scripture. Consider how the Old Testament story in which we laid our foundation will skyrocket us to the very words of Jesus Christ, who said in the Sermon on the Mount, "For where your treasure is, there your heart will be also" (Matthew 6:21). He continues, "The eye"—there's that word again, so, bear in mind the vocabulary available at that time to describe heretofore unrealized concepts, such as the subconscious—"is the lamp of the body. If your eyes are healthy, your whole body will be full of light. But if your eyes are unhealthy, your whole body will be full of darkness" (Matthew 6:22-23).

I'm a lover of the Word of God. Words are important; they are the seeds we have at our disposal to create anything we want in our lives. In Genesis, the author writes that God "spoke you and I into existence."

In the early days of CrossFit, Coach was faced with a bit of a predicament because he was claiming that CrossFit was teaching people "functional movement." Instructors made pilgrimages from all over the world to visit CrossFit and they had their own definitions of the term. In fact, everyone seemed to have laid claim to the term despite their very different training regimens.

Coach realized he needed to redefine his terminology. The term "functional movement" is useless if everyone is using it to describe something different.

Therefore, returning to the words from the Sermon on the Mount in Matthew, you'll see that they, too, are important to examine for their meaning. Consider these words: "eye," "lamp," and "body."

"Eye" derives from the Greek "*ophthalmos*," which, in addition to the physical qualities of the eye, also included the faculty of knowing. That information certainly provides some context for our story of Elisha, as well as illuminating the words of Jesus when he says, "The eye is the lamp of the body."

So, when Jesus goes on to say, "If your eye is healthy, your whole body will be full of light" (Matthew 6:22), I think it's fair to say he's using the second definition of the word, referring to the quality of the mind.

To continue, "light" comes from the Greek word "*phōteinos*." The Hebrew equivalent of that word first appears in the Bible in the creation story of Genesis. When God created light, the Hebrew word used is "*ōre.*" Jesus will interchange the words for light, switching between "*phōteinos*" and "*lychnos*," which is a candle stand or lamp stand. If the lamp is the mind, consider the implications of what might be meant by a lamp *stand*. Is that not an apt description of the body's role? The word "body" has its roots in the Greek "*soma.*" A biblical mentor of mine and expert in New Testament Greek, offered an amazing definition of *soma* that it is "that which casts a shadow *as distinguished from the shadow itself.*"

Jesus seems to be revealing something very important to us. Allow me a moment to strengthen this concept for you.

Phōteinos, much like the light of the sun, when it hits our body, (or *soma*), would potentially cast a shadow. Therefore, at the supernatural and metaphysical level, to say that the "eye is the lamp of the body" would imply that the quality of *phos* (representing our thinking) directly influences the quality of the *soma* (representing the physical experience of our thinking). Strictly speaking, the physical reality of our life is simply the effect, the cause of which was created in our mind. Therefore, the quality of our body (our *soma*—referring to the health and wellness of our physical body) and the "totality of the body" we experience in life can be directly influenced by the quality of our thinking.

In other words, your mind projects your reality.

Returning to the essential truths, the second is that our thinking influences the quality of what we see. Jesus goes on to say, "You are the light of the world. A town built on a hill cannot be hidden. You have heard it said to the people long ago" (Matthew 5:14; 21). What he's doing when he says, "You have heard it said to the people long ago" (Matthew 5:21) is reminding the reader of the words of the Old Testament. Jesus continues, "You shall not murder, and anyone who murders will be subject to judgment. But I tell you that anyone who is angry with a brother or sister will be subject to judgment. Therefore, if you are offering your gift at the altar and there remember that your brother or sister has something against you, leave your gift in front of the altar. First go and be reconciled to them, then come back and offer your gift" (Matthew 5:22-24).

Take that one piece at a time. I want to extract the words, "altar" and "gift." I propose that "altar" represents the consciousness and that "gift" is a prayer or any thought. So, what Jesus is saying is that in the Old Testament, before someone brought a gift—a tangible offering, such as a lamb—to the altar of God, there was significant ritual that required accomplishing. The person had to be *clean* before offering a gift.

Jesus references the implications of the Old Testament, reminding them they've heard it said that in the days of old before you offered your gift, you had to be clean. If they were not clean, they couldn't offer the gift. If they weren't pure, neither would the gift be.

But this is taking place in the context of a discussion about murder: "You've heard it said, you shall not commit murder" (Matthew 5:21; cf. Exodus 20:13). What was murder? A *physical* act. Yet Jesus is proposing something profound. He seems to be saying, "If you don't commit murder but you have anger in your mind for your brother and sister, you are still subject to judgment." So, why would he equate the physical act of murder with anger in the mind? The answer lies in the fact that he has just said that the "eye is the lamp of the body." Thus, if anger was harbored in the mind—or jealousy or adulterous thoughts or any other sin—it would find expression.

Why is that the case? The key is in the words, "You are the light of the world. A town built on a hill cannot be hidden." The "town built on a hill," is an apt description of *consciousness*. So, in other words, you cannot hide your consciousness. In time, everything that you think will be revealed. Jesus knew that in time, if anger was harbored in the mind, it would express itself. Thus, it all makes sense now when he ties in the idea of purifying yourself. He's saying, "Before you think, purify yourself."

In fact, we now know that anger—and jealousy, as well as other emotions— do find expression in the physical body. Whether it's anger or jealousy you're feeling, Jesus is warning that that's a danger. And if you find that you're harboring anger, you simply need to ask God to purify your "heart."

The third essential truth, the fact that the quality of our thinking can be improved by resting in the presence of God, will be illuminated by a beautiful prayer written by one of my favorite biblical heroes: David. The Bible says that he was beloved by God because he had a *heart* for God (1 Samuel 13:14; Acts 13:22). Based on the above, it should be becoming clear that the Bible isn't referring to the cardiopulmonary organ in his chest.

As he neared the end of his life, David wrote a lot of Psalms, composing more than half of them during this reflective period. He even reveals to us that it was not his own strength that enabled him to defeat the giant Goliath. As he charged his foe, slinging a killing stone, he yelled, "I come to you in the name of the LORD Almighty" (1 Samuel 17:45). Notice he didn't say, "I come to you on the basis of my training and experience."

He writes in Psalm 51:10, "Create in me a clean heart, O God, and put a new and right spirit within me." In this prayer, it's clear that David understands the power of his mind and is asking for a clear mind, that the quality of his thinking be elevated. That's a crucial matter in light of the fact that in his younger years he squared off with what was essentially a monster. So, just as Elisha saw the *actuality* of the battlefield situation, David is now asking God for that same clarity, so that he can be confident in the knowledge that "the forces that are for me are greater than the forces that are against me."

I believe Psalm 51:10 can be life-changing. When you become aware that the quality of your thinking has become fearful, anxious, or negative, recite the prayer that David prayed in Psalm 51:10.

—— *FEARFULLY & WONDERFULLY MADE* ——

As a DEA agent, I had an opportunity to test for the DEA FAST (Foreign-deployed Advisory and Support Team) team, essentially the Federal equivalent of a domestic police SWAT team and the pinnacle of what I felt my career would be. I'd previously served on a SWAT team with the Santa Cruz County Sheriff's office and absolutely loved it. There's a great saying in law enforcement that when the cops need help, they call SWAT. One of my all-time favorite Hollywood lines comes from the movie, SWAT: "You're either SWAT or you're not."

Needless to say, when my opportunity arrived, I said to myself, "Yes, where do I sign up? How can I join the team?" Well, it turns out joining the team is no easy task. It would require thirty days of assessment and selection at DEA headquarters in Quantico, Virginia.

I did some research on the expectations of the team and the type of testing evolutions they would do during what would be the hardest crucible of my entire life. It turned out several evolutions and training scenarios would involve navigating obstacles from significant height, one of which would be fast-roping from helicopters. That posed a major problem because at that time, I was terrified of heights.

I knew someone, however, who was very confident at heights and would be able to mentor and train me for these upcoming evolutions. I called my dear friend Mark Divine, a then-twenty-year Navy SEAL who went on to found the SEALFIT program, which has a resounding success rate in helping candidates succeed in any special operations endeavor. I knew that my best chance of success during the assessment and selection would be spending as much time as possible in Mark's company.

I called and asked if he could help me. He said, "Of course. Meet me in Coronado at the Navy SEAL compound this Saturday."

That Saturday morning, I drove up very early from my El Centro residence, right on the border. Two hours later, I was standing tall at the Navy SEAL compound, anticipating a safety brief, with Mark providing me with some points of performance on how to navigate obstacles at height. But, oh no, that was not to be. Instead, in a booming voice, Mark spoke the two words that ring true for any leader, "Follow me."

He took off in a dead sprint through the soft sand toward the Navy

SEAL obstacle course and led me right at a cargo net. Even though we were approximately a mile away, this cargo net seemed to be reaching into the sky. It just seemed so vast, so tall. And the closer we got, the taller it continued to appear.

As we approached, I hoped that Mark would slow down and provide me with some points of performance, some clues, some tips, some strategy, some technique, something to help boost my morale and confidence and courage. But, again, that was not to be. He actually sped up.

As he approached the obstacle, he said once again, "follow me!" And up he began to climb. I did my best to climb next to him up to the very top. And there we stopped.

Now, at the top of the cargo net, there was about a two-foot gap between the very top of the rope and a large wooden beam that looked similar to a telephone pole. I hoped that we would simply climb back down the same way we went up but, of course, that was not to be.

"All right Greg," he said, "now, I want you to climb up and over that wooden beam and down the other side."

I completely froze in that moment. I bored down on that rope full-grip, as strong as I possibly could, as if my life depended on that rope and my ability to hang onto it. Mark looked at me and said in a very calm voice, "Greg, this would be a great time to take a breath."

And then and there, in my early thirties, I took the first conscious breath of my entire life.

I was a CrossFit athlete and a DEA agent, I had served in the military and on a sheriff's SWAT team. Yet, all that athletic and tactical training was for naught at this moment in my life because none of that training had emphasized the importance of breath awareness.

That first conscious breath changed my life. I became fully present in that instant. The result of that one amazing breath was that I relaxed my grip. I'm not referring to my physical stranglehold on the rope; I mean my mental grip on fear. I released my grip just a little bit. Unfortunately, that release didn't last long. The next thing Mark said was, "Okay, climb up over the beam." I locked up tightly again.

Yet again, Mark said something profound: "Point to the cause of the stress."

I took another deep breath and located the source of my stress: my mind. My thoughts about that immediate moment in space and time were fear-inducing. That knowledge was a breakthrough for me because what I realized was that

I was defeating myself. If my thinking could prevent me from doing something that I actually wanted to do, my thinking could just as easily serve me by setting me up for success.

What a gift Mark had given me. I very consciously took a breath and said to myself, "I can do it. I believe in myself. I've got this." I looked confidently at Mark and said, "Hooyah." Then, up and over that beam I went, safely down the other side. He and I continued to run multiple evolutions, tackling all the obstacles on the course.

In a matter of hours, I had conquered my terrifying fear of heights, changing my life forever. The bizarre feature of that fear was that it was entirely irrational, there were no height-related incidents in my youth that substantiated such fear. I was only afraid of heights because, for whatever reason, I believed I was afraid of heights. And when I went up and over the beam, the fear disappeared.

Now, did I have a healthy respect for heights? Absolutely. But after that moment, I made an oath to myself that in situations involving heights, I would use my thinking only to serve me in overcoming the obstacle.

As Mark and I wrapped up that physical training, he gave me a word of advice that I carry close to my heart to this day. I've passed on this word of advice in a variety of contexts to family, friends, loved ones, and now to you. Mark said, "Stay the course, Greg." And so I say to you, "Stay the course."

I have come to understand the real meaning of the wisdom in those three simple words. In order to stay the course, you must stand your ground. The common thread of "stay" and "stand" is that they are in the present tense. Whether you're staying or standing, you, too, must be present.

Our minds possess the power to project into the uncertainty of the future and to regress into memories of the past. Even while our bodies are locked into the here-and-now, our thoughts may be somewhere else entirely. In order to be successful and reach our fullest potential, we must firmly plant both the mind and body into the fertile soil of the present moment.

Andy Rios, a phenomenal SWAT operator, and Andy Stumpf, both of whom are dear friends and former Navy SEALs, confirm this idea of staying in the present moment when faced with any semblance of a challenge.

In *Firebreather Fitness*, I extensively researched micro-goals and the power of staying in the present moment. Part of that research involved speaking at great length with Andy Stumpf, who shared with me a strategy he used while going though Navy SEAL BUD/S—the epic, grueling endurance-training program required to become a SEAL. What Andy did in the context of micro-goals and staying present is remarkable: he never set a goal more than about four hours into the future!

I asked him why he chose a four-hour timeline. He laughed and said, "Well, that was the time of the next meal." In other words, Andy simply was setting a micro-goal and that goal was, "I'm going to make it to the next meal." Then, as he was enjoying the meal, he would set his next four-hour goal: "I am going to make it to the next goal." In his case, that meant the next meal.

It's a very powerful principle in that his micro-goal was never more than four hours out of reach.

For those of us participating in the sport of CrossFit, a micro-goal could simply be the next repetition. In some of the really emotionally challenging moments of my life, such as the loss of my mother or father, my micro-goal was simply the next breath. That's as micro as we can go; simply to live from one breath to the next.

To delve that deep into the present moment is not to surrender. You're not lying down and giving up. In fact, you are welcoming the presence of God into your life. Recall that before the spirit was formed in you, God had to breathe the breath of life into your body. Therefore, every time you breathe, if that is, in fact, the most micro level we can reduce to, breath-to-breath is a very potent place to exist.

Mark gave me still another piece of advice, rather open-ended, that helped shape my life: "Greg, there's bound to be some times in that course when you are going to question your resolve. How about writing yourself a letter?"

That afternoon, as I drove the two hours on I-10 back to El Centro, I thought to myself, "That's exactly what I need to do." I realized I needed to write myself a letter because I'd be doing so in the present moment, when I would be clear on my intention to be successful in the assesment course. Therefore, if a moment arose on the course when my mind wanted to retreat to the past or project into the future, I would have an anchor to keep myself in the present.

Scripture teaches the importance of an anchor for the soul. I decided to anchor my soul, my intention, my commitment by writing myself a letter. And if during the course I were to experience doubt or uncertainty, I could solidly reaffirm my ability to succeed by reading my letter. That's exactly what I did.

When I got back, I went right to my desk and typed myself out a letter, which I printed and neatly folded inside an ID cardholder that I wore in a lanyard. I put it in upside down so that when I flipped it up it from around my neck it would be right side up.

That letter impacted me so much that I still have it these many years later. That exact letter went with me for thirty days in which I read it often, sometimes several times a day. It's now framed and in front of me as I write. In fact, I'm going to share this letter with you now:

> Greg, remember when you read this, where you have been and what you have done and what you have learned and how you have helped others. The decision to test for FAST was a decision you made. You made this decision because you believed in yourself. You believed in your ability to succeed and you believed in your ability to encourage others to succeed as well. You can do it. You will always know in your heart you had the courage to attempt something challenging, difficult, strenuous, and demanding. God is with you, Greg. God is helping you. Be at your best every day. Greg, above all, remember this: through Christ, you can do all things. You are brave. You are a warrior. You can do it.

That's a powerful letter. And I feel absolutely certain, I have conviction that the Holy Spirit moved through me as I wrote this letter to myself. What God inspired me to write to myself was in the service of other people. Therefore, there's a quality within this letter that I wrote to myself that essentially speaks to you, the reader, right now. Notice that I wrote that I believed in my ability to encourage others to succeed, as well.

One of the great lessons Mark and his amazing staff taught me during the epic crucible of Kokoro camp is that when we take our eyes off ourselves and put them on our teammate, we are blessed twice, because as we help others, we allow the karmic benefit of cause-and-effect to work in our favor; as we turn our attention away from our suffering to focus on encouraging, helping, supporting, loving, and motivating another person, we allow the universe to reciprocate that action and quality in our favor.

In other words, as we take the time and effort to help someone else, someone else takes the time and effort to help us. It's the law of the universe, which God created.

Furthermore, when we take our eyes and our attention off our own suffering, the suffering takes its attention away from us.

I taught a CrossFit goal-setting course for years and one of the laws that I encouraged people to abide by was this: that which you focus your attention on will increase in your life. Therefore, if you focus on your suffering, you are going to experience a lot of suffering. But if you focus on loving, encouraging, supporting, benefiting, and being a blessing to others, you'll receive love, encouragement, support, and so on. We get what we give.

Notice, too, that I referenced Scripture in my letter. I knew that I would need the support of the Holy Spirit; I would need the presence of God in my life during that course. In writing, "Above all of that Greg, remember this: Through Christ, you can do all things" I was referencing the Bible verse found in Philippians 4:13. That's so important to understand. If we're trying to navigate the ebb and flow of life on our own, ultimately, we will never reach our full potential. However, when we navigate that ebb and flow with the support, the presence, and the strength of Jesus Christ, then and only then, will we be able to accomplish our dreams, our goals, our mission, and our very purpose in life.

I encourage you to do what I did. Follow the advice that Mark gave me; write yourself a letter. If you have a goal, if you have a challenge in your life, if you have a dream, I want you to write yourself a letter. It doesn't matter if it's in pen or pencil or typed out. Make a commitment to yourself. There is something very, very powerful when you express what is in your mind as words on a page. It becomes very tangible, it becomes very real, it becomes that anchor for your soul.

I want to share with you a Bible verse that I encourage you to commit to memory. It's from the Book of Psalms. Remember that the majority of Psalms was written by one my biblical heroes, David—as in David and Goliath—one of the greatest warrior kings of all time. He writes, "I am fearfully and wonderfully made" (Psalms 139:14).

What a beautiful Bible verse to commit to memory to remember that God made you and me in His image. And what image is that? An image that is fearfully and wonderfully made. Now the word "wonderfully" can speak for itself. The word "fearfully," however, takes some greater understanding.

The Bible often uses the word "fear" in relation to our experience of God. To fear God, biblically speaking, is a great blessing on one's self, to experience the presence of God with fear. It's crucial to understand the context of "fear" to better appreciate what the Psalmist is encouraging us to experience in our relationship to our self, to our own image.

The fear of God is multifaceted. To fear God means to respect, appreciate, honor, and revere God, the all-powerful Creator of the universe, who is worthy of our love, respect and, of course, our fear. Yet it's not fear in the sense that we would fear a bully or, in my case, heights. It is a fear from a place of love, as we are in such admiration, awe, and astonishment of the power of God that we fear out of love. We respect the power, the authority of our Father in Heaven. It's within that context that the Psalmist encourages us to utilize this great piece of Scripture.

Therefore, when you commit to memory and repeat within the temple of your mind, "I am fearfully and wonderfully made," what you're proposing to your subconscious mind is that you are powerful, worthy of respect and admiration.

Now, when we layer this Psalm from the Old Testament onto the New Testament's "I can do all things through Christ who strengthens me," we really have a beautiful razor-sharp, double-edged sword to wield, which can cut through any self-doubt, anxiety, uncertainty, nervousness, or fear. Swinging the sword one way, I am fearfully and wonderfully made. Swinging it the other, I realize that the respect, admiration, and wonder I have in my creation is substantiated on the life of Jesus Christ.

I hope these ideas bring you encouragement. In the words of my friend and mentor, Mark Divine, "Stay the course." Stay in the present moment. Stand your ground. You are fearfully and wonderfully made. Right now, in this moment, as you take the next breath, my friends, know that the presence of God is with you.

Remember, you are made in the image of God: "You can do all things through Christ who strengthens you" (Philippians 4:13). You are brave. You are courageous. You are a warrior. And, my friends, I believe you can do it.

SPIRITUAL PRACTICE IN THE WARRIOR TRADITION

In the early days of CrossFit, I would travel with Coach to start-up CrossFit affiliate gyms in preparation for a seminar. Coach would insist on arriving a day early to recon the gym, feel the energy of the space, and conduct impromptu tests for what he referred to as "Principles of Alignment." What he taught me significantly shaped my life and guided the practices at CrossFit Amundson.

I remember peeking through a window of a CrossFit affiliate gym with Coach. The owners and athletes had long since returned home and the gym was empty. Coach said to me, "Hey kid, see that? Look at those bumper plates and tell me what you see."

I put my face up to the glass window and peered inside. I saw a stack of black forty-five-pound plates stacked against a wall. Nothing looked out of place or out of the ordinary.

"Yeah, so what? Some black plates," I replied.

"See how they are not stacked neatly? How there is no alignment? If a gym owner can't properly align bumper plates, I question their ability to align their clients' backs. Attention to detail is everything."

I was blown away. Coach was exactly right. As I looked again at the plates, I saw what he had referred to. There was no order, no alignment, no attention to detail. We train in physical disciplines to develop a set of principles and then apply those principles throughout our entire lives. A principle by its very nature is universal; it does not apply in a vacuum. Rather, it's a guiding light in our lives, helping to create order, alignment, and focus in our life.

A spiritual practice requires aligning our principles with our actions. We create alignment in life by continually adjusting our thoughts, words, and actions to be consistent with our principles.

— SPIRITUAL DISCIPLINES: THE KEY TO VICTORY —

"Discipline yourself for the purpose of godliness."
—1 Timothy 4:7

As an NCAA Division-III competitive water polo player at the University of California at Santa Cruz, I was often at the mercy of coaches who insisted on the benefits of practice before the sun came up. As a college student in my twenties, cold and dark early mornings on the pool deck were not particularly congruent with the preferred lifestyle of a young adult. My friends were staying out late and enjoying leisurely mornings of coffee and bagels, while my teammates and I were busy doing pool-deck gymnastic exercises, relentless drills, and endless laps in the swimming pool.

Coach McGregor, the head coach and authority on both water polo and young-adult leadership, would constantly remind me, "This is what it takes to be a winner! You've got to have more discipline than your opponent."

He would reinforce within my mind the vision of what I was working so hard for. He helped me see myself as successful, both in sport and in life. His ability to inspire vision within me provided context for the discipline he demanded from me.

I recall one early morning on the pool deck Coach McGregor said something that accelerated my maturity and positive trajectory in life: "Anything you do once or twice a week is just a hobby. In order for it to become discipline, you've got to do it every day of your life."

"Anything you do once or twice a week is just a hobby. In order for it to become discipline, you've got to do it every day of your life."
—Coach McGregor

As important as discipline was for me as a young athlete, the greater implications of "disciplining myself for the purpose of godliness" (1 Timothy 4:7) have become the most important use of my mind, body, and spirit, as I train to "increase in wisdom, stature, and favor with God and mankind" (Luke 2:52).

I feel confident that you will have the same realization and experience as you embark upon the training program I have prepared for you in *Victory*.

DEFINING THE SPIRITUAL DISCIPLINES

Spiritual disciplines differ from *worldly* disciplines in their focus upon *eternal* growth rather than *temporal* growth. When Jesus Christ spoke of "storing up treasure in heaven" (Matthew 6:20), he was pointing his disciples to eternity, helping them differentiate between the temporal matters of the world and the eternal priority of the Kingdom of God. "Store your treasures in heaven, where moths and rust cannot destroy and thieves do not break in and steal. Wherever your treasure is, there the desires of your heart will also be" (Matthew 6:19-20).

The spiritual disciplines are God's way of ensuring His children can "press toward the goal for the prize of the upward call of God in Christ Jesus" (Philippians 3:13-14). They involve deliberate and intentional training and practice, with the specific purpose of increasing in godliness. The spiritual disciplines are the means God has given us to train to live as Jesus Christ did, and are intended to help form the character and mind of Christ within us. They are the "habits of devotion and experiential Christianity" that have been practiced by individuals and congregations since biblical times and are "the only road to Christian maturity and godliness" as prescribed by the Word of God.[15]

Brian Hedges is one of my favorite Christian authors. He writes, "Jesus did not possess any special means of spiritual growth which are not available to us. It is essential to realize this if we are to understand Jesus and if we are to become like him."[16]

Recalling my experience in discipline for the purpose of athleticism, one consistent attribute of great professional athletes was the amount of time they spent each day in the pursuit of mastering their sport. In the same manner, the duration of time spent within the practice of spiritual disciplines is of immense importance. As with any relationship, I have discovered that the best way for me to gain increased intimacy with God is to spend time with Him. Spending time with God requires setting aside specific blocks of time each day for the sole purpose of practicing the spiritual disciplines.

In athletic training, very often a significant amount of sheer willpower is needed to simply *get to the gym*. However, once inside the "gym space," set aside for the purpose of athletic development, the athlete is then able to begin the respective practices of their sport with greater focus, intensity, and efficiency. Similarly, the use of silence and solitude serve the purpose of creating a "holy space," where the spiritual disciplines can be practiced much easier.

For my personal training with the spiritual disciplines, I have dedicated a small section of my living room to the sole purpose of communion with God. The moment I step into my "holy space" to connect with God, I feel the Holy Spirit transforming me "like a tree planted by streams of water, which yields its fruit in season and whose leaf does not wither" (Psalm 1:3).

Reflecting on the words of the Psalmist, "Oh, how I love your law! I meditate on it *all day long*" (Psalm 119:97), I have found that as my time in the spiritual disciplines increases, the Word of God tends to play like background music in my mind throughout the entire day. As the Word of God circulates throughout my mind on an increasingly consistent basis, I have full confidence in the direction and promise of the Apostle Paul to "not conform to the pattern of this world but be transformed by the renewing of your mind" (Romans 12:2).

In my practice of the spiritual disciplines, I have discovered that the disciplines of silence and solitude are the "gateway personal disciplines" that create physical, environmental, and mental "holy space" for the other spiritual disciplines to shape my life.

Furthermore, I have found that the *quality* of time spent with God is far more important than the *quantity* of time. And perhaps most importantly, I have happily discovered that unlike the sheer effort and use of individual willpower required in the worldly application of discipline, the spiritual disciplines differ because their effectiveness depends on the gracious work of the Spirit of God.

I am happy and grateful to introduce to you the eight spiritual disciplines that have had the greatest influence on my life, in addition to the lives of the thousands of athletes I have been blessed to train and mentor.

"Be transformed by the renewing of your mind."

—Romans 12:2

Professional boxer Robert "The Ghost" Guerrero and I use the spiritual disciplines on a regular basis when we train together.

— MY EIGHT ESSENTIAL SPIRITUAL DISCIPLINES —

1. FORGIVENESS AND INNER PEACE — THE KEY TO SELF MASTERY

My dad was an amazing man and has been the most influential person in my life. He was a Navy diver, beach lifeguard, champion swimmer and bodybuilder, world-renowned doctor of chiropractic, energetic healer, chaplain, and pastor. One of the key spiritual principles he preached and instilled in my life was the power of *forgiveness*. He explained it to me this way: "Forgiveness is, in fact, a daily practice of acceptance for what is. Whether you call it 'forgiving' or 'being at peace with,' the power the practice holds in our life is immense."

My friend Rolf Gates once told me, "A spiritual practice is the discipline of bringing into alignment your values and actions." I contemplated and meditated upon this statement for several days and then reflected on what my dad had taught me about the power of forgiveness. I realized that one of my daily spiritual practices, as defined by Rolf, was disciplining myself to be aware of thoughts that needed to be forgiven, released, and, ultimately, replaced.

Every time you face a life event, you have what could be referred to as "free agency" or "choice" as to how you will think, and resultantly, feel and respond to the situation. The situation does not necessarily need to be something you see externally or something that "happens" to you. Very often, the greatest stressors in life are in the form of your own thoughts.

My friend and expert martial artist and combat instructor Tony Blauer taught me years ago that "FEAR" really means "False Evidence Appearing Real." In the context of a self-defense situation, therefore, any internal fear you feel about your opponent exists solely in your mind. When you overcome your mind, you can much more easily overcome any challenge set before you.

One of the most empowering realizations you can achieve in life is the certainty that you always retain choice about how you will react to trials and tribulations. In other words, it is not our circumstances and life events that define us. Instead, it is our individual *thinking about the events* that ultimately shapes the quality of our life experience.

Furthermore, as I taught for years in the CrossFit goal-setting course, "When we change the way we look at something, what we look at begins to change."

When we feel overwhelmed, our thinking and behavior degenerates from constructive to destructive, from creative to self-defeating. We procrastinate, lose motivation, curiosity, and enthusiasm. The feelings of stress that are generated by self-defeating thoughts in the mind (as Mark Divine would say, "feeding the wolf of fear") lead to confusion, uncertainty, fatigue, and depression. Worse, it lowers our auto-immune system, often resulting in illness and disease.

This is where the wisdom, revelation, and incredible work of my dad, Dr. Raymond Amundson, can greatly benefit our spiritual practice and growth. My dad was a deeply spiritual man who taught his patients how to "forgive with love." He believed many people suffered mentally and physically due to an accumulation of stress and lack of peace in their lives. He taught me that in order to live a life free of stress, I had to pursue a life filled with inner peace. Rather than attempting to resist stress, which would only lead to more stress, I had to focus my mind on God and, through His grace, I would then achieve deep inner peace.

When it comes to forgiveness, I go back to my dad's way of thinking about the purpose of chiropractic adjustments: as a means letting light and love flow through the body. Forgiveness is like an adjustment for the body and mind, as well. It has the power to "crack open" the self-imposed chains of anger, pride, fear, self-doubt, insecurity, and grief that can wreak physical and emotional havoc on our lives.

My dad taught that the state of being at peace requires three things:

1. Living up to our value standards;
2. Righting our wrongs; and
3. Forgiving, forgiving, forgiving.

Value standards are the fundamental beliefs we hold as true. My dad taught me that a value standard is like a north-pointing compass or a lighthouse in the dark—a guidance tool. Our value standards are an inseparable part of who we are, how we think, and what we believe to be right and wrong. He also emphasized that it was vital that our value standards be in alignment with the Word of God.

When an event does not conform to our value standards, the result is stress. For example, one of the value standards I was taught as a young boy was kindness. In the seventh grade, I experienced that up close and personal when I was bullied and kneed in the groin by a bully; it was a combination of the physical pain he caused, coupled with the mental stress associated with accepting the violation of a personal value standard.

The real enemy, therefore, was not the bully, but my internal thoughts about the bully. Only by forgiving the bully—and forgiving myself for the feelings of fear, insecurity, and helplessness—could I move forward with my life. The principle of forgiving the act, forgiving others, and forgiving ourselves, is a daily act of discipline and faith, and in itself, is a profound spiritual practice.

The essence of forgiveness takes many titles, ranging from "non-attachment" to "non-judgment." However, at the end of the day, it boils down to an ability to release the negative charge with your feelings about yourself, another person, or a life circumstance. Just like Coach taught me all those years ago: the greatest adaptation really does take place between our ears.

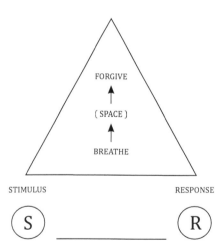

The diagram above is a visual representation of the steps to effectively using forgiveness. Between "STIMULUS" and "RESPONSE" we can take a breath, create space, and forgive. The practice of breathing, creating space, and forgiving allows for the transcendence of life circumstances and enhances our ability to make loving choices about our thoughts, words, and actions.

Forgiveness is a powerful act we can use at the intersection of *stimulus* and *response*. When we combine conscious breathing with forgiveness, we empower ourselves by calming the turbulence in our lives and silencing what warriors refer to as our "monkey mind," the incessant, non-productive, and often harmful mind-chatter. In the space between our thoughts and actions, we can take a breath and forgive.

The powerful act of forgiveness is the first step in releasing the grasp of the past. Forgiveness also provides us with the space we need in our mind to choose loving thoughts, words, and actions that will positively shape our future.

These are the three steps to the effective use of forgiveness:

1. Speak aloud the specific act you are forgiving in yourself or another person;

2. If your words or actions negatively affected another person, ask them to forgive you;

3. The power of forgiveness is multiplied when we forgive in the presence of a loved one, such as a spouse, parent, brother, sister, or friend.

Pursuing a life of peace is, therefore, a matter of identifying our value standards and upholding them. We must develop the courage to choose the hard right over the easy wrong, and practice using forgiveness to transcend our mistakes and the mistakes of others.

Sometimes, the simplest acts have the most profound impact on our lives. I encourage you to bring the pursuit of peace and the practice of forgiveness into your life.

GUIDELINE TO MANAGING STRESS & FINDING PEACE

1. **LOVE YOURSELF.** Write a list of all the things you love about yourself: commendable character traits, personal qualities that are admirable, respected personality traits, accomplishments, talents, and unique ways of doing things and seeing the world. This is not a brag sheet, rather, it is a personal assessment and way of building self-esteem. The Second Great Commandment says to love your neighbor as yourself (Mark 12:31), not *in spite of* or *instead of* yourself. The only way to really love another person is to love yourself.

2. **FORGIVE QUICKLY.** Discipline yourself to act immediately. Don't let it fester for even a minute. Remember the words of Jesus Christ: "But of you, it is required to forgive all men" (Matthew 6:14).

THE ACTION STEPS TO FORGIVENESS

1. **FORGIVE OUT LOUD.** This is extremely effective. You *need* to hear yourself say it and feel it.

2. **BE SPECIFIC.** Name who you are forgiving and what you are forgiving them for.

3. **USE THE PRESENT TENSE.** Your statement should begin, "I forgive..." rather than, "I can forgive" or "I'd like to forgive," etc.

4. **BE SINCERE.** Remember, every time you think of what offended you, you've got to forgive it again.

5. **LOVE OTHERS.** Write of your love for your spouse, family members, and friends. Be liberal and specific in your compliments of other people. Be kind, loving, and encouraging. Adhere to the concept of BUIYATAOO (Believe Unconditionally In Yourself And The Ability Of Others).

6. **DO RIGHT.** Discipline yourself to live up to your personal value standards. This is the meaning of integrity—a warrior virtue. Discipline yourself to be a person of excellence. Do the right thing even when nobody is watching.

7. **EXPRESS FEELINGS OF GRATITUDE.** Be grateful for everyone and everything. Even life situations you originally thought of as unwanted or challenging, when reframed and viewed with gratitude, open the way for developing personal strength. When you adopt the mindset that *everything* that you experience is for your good, your life will change in a profoundly positive way.

8. **BE AT PEACE.** Use forgiveness to achieve peace with yourself and others.

FORGIVENESS IN "REAL LIFE"

A few months before he was to be deployed to Vietnam as a Navy Officer on a thirty-one-foot Navy river patrol boat, my dad severely injured his right eye during a Naval scuba diving accident in San Diego. As a result of his injury, his position as commander of the boat was forfeited to another officer and he was reassigned to a different post.

Three months after arriving in Vietnam and starting to patrol the dangerous waterways of the Mekong Delta, the boat my dad would have commanded was ambushed by an enemy platoon. Everyone aboard was killed.

My dad said he was deeply depressed for several months afterward, believing that he should have been on the boat. He believed his presence could have saved the lives of his men.

Only through prayer and forgiveness was he able to transcend the loss of his friends, and his feelings of failure, anger, guilt, and grief. At the moment of forgiveness, however, a brilliant light opened in his heart and mind. Only a few short weeks later, my dad met my mom, sparking a thirty-year relationship that included my birth and the birth of my brothers.

My dad went on to become a doctor of chiropractic, with one of the most successful practices in the country. He developed and taught a form of chiropractic care based on the tenants of spirituality and forgiveness.

That lesson from my dad's own life experience has helped me through many of my own challenges. Our circumstances may appear to overwhelm us in the moment. It is in these moments that we must learn to retain faith in ourselves, in other people, and most importantly, in our God. In addition, we must remember that our thoughts about what happens in our life are far more important than what *actually* happens.

2. SOLITUDE AND SILENCE

Brian Hedges writes, "The spiritual disciplines are about being with God and about cultivating a relationship with Him."[17] I have found that in order to "be with God," I need to create time and space each day for solitude and silence in His mighty presence.

One of the most encouraging Bible verses I have found that substantiates the combined spiritual disciplines of solitude and silence is, "Let him sit alone [solitude] in silence [refraining from speech] for the LORD has laid it on him" (Lamentations 3:28).[18]

As with all spiritual disciplines, it is of the utmost importance to remember their purpose, which is "disciplining oneself for the purpose of godliness" (1 Timothy 4:7). Therefore, as one of my favorite seminary professors, Dr. Wiggins of Western Seminary, pointed out in a lecture on the combined spiritual disciplines of slowing, silence, solitude and rest, "Solitude and silence are not simply practiced to avoid people but, rather, to avoid the distractions that keep us from hearing God." [19]

In modeling the life of Jesus Christ, there are numerous examples of our Lord's demonstration of the importance of solitude and silence. In particular, I have found great inspiration in the account of Luke 1:35, when early in the morning, "Jesus got up, left the house, and went off to a solitary place, where he prayed."

In my personal practice of the combined disciplines of solitude and silence, I start each morning in a very consistent manner. I take comfort in routine and begin each day by awakening before the sunrise and sitting silently in the presence of God. I have happily discovered that intimacy with God will always be found in the present moment. Therefore, as I sit in silence and solitude in the expansive presence of God, I direct my attention to the present moment and invite the Holy Spirit to "create within me a clean heart O God, and put a new and right spirit within me" (Psalm 51:10).

A WARRIOR TRADITION STORY ON STILLNESS

In the small farming village of Kanto of ancient Japan, there lived three well-known samurai warriors and an elder monk respected throughout the entire countryside. A tribe of ruthless bandits threatened to destroy the village.

With an attack looming, the old monk decided to hold a test to determine which of the three samurai would have responsibility for protecting the village. He had a servant arm himself with a longsword, hide behind the doorway of a village hut, and cut down anyone who entered.

He then instructed the three samurai on his challenge: "Enter this doorway and display all your knowledge, technique, and ability in the martial ways."

The first samurai drew his sword and rushed through the doorway. The waiting servant quickly cut him down.

The second samurai also drew his sword and entered the doorway. He was more aware of his surroundings, however, and was able to anticipate the attack and, thus, avoid death.

The third samurai did not even draw his sword. He waited outside the doorway and stood very still. He then closed his eyes and took a long, slow, deep breath. "You, inside the doorway," he said. "Come out and surrender or you will surely be destroyed."

Upon hearing this, the servant exited the doorway.

Having witnessed the entire sequence of events, the elder monk proclaimed to the third samurai, "You are the one who shall save our village."

3. MEDITATION

As I mentioned in Part One, meditation for the purpose of spiritual growth has been a tremendously powerful daily practice in my life. But I now want to distinguish between meditation as I presented it in the section that dealt with the mind and here, as it pertains to the spirit.

The Psalmist wrote, "Blessed is the one whose delight is in the law of the LORD and who meditates on His law day and night" (Psalm 1:2). It is extremely important to note that meditation for the purpose of godliness differs from other types of meditation, which might focus on *emptying* the mind. The type of meditation encouraged in the Bible advocates *filling* the mind with the Word of

God. As the Apostle Paul wrote in Philippians, the purpose of Christian meditation is to help our mind focus upon "whatever is true, whatever is noble, whatever is right, whatever is pure, whatever is lovely, whatever is admirable—if anything is excellent or praiseworthy—think about such things" (Philippians 4:8).

> ### Christian meditation could be described as the intent to evenly expand the Word of God across one's entire mind.

In my practice of meditation for the purpose of godliness, I have found great benefit in repeating a Bible verse within my mind as a continuation of my spiritual practice of solitude, silence, and Bible intake.

In addition to repeating Scripture and the mantra "I AM," which I teach in *The Warrior and The Monk*, I have also found the "Jesus Christ Prayer" has been a wonderful way to achieve greater intimacy with God and peace in His awesome presence.[20]

With my eyes closed, the spiritual disciplines of solitude and silence naturally create the needed "holy space," which draws me into the practice of meditation. I have found the most benefit from a twenty-minute meditation first thing in the morning and another twenty-minute period of meditation, solitude, and silence in the afternoon at approximately 3PM (Reference Acts 3:1).

Often, the meditative period in the afternoon is such a sharp contrast from the hurriedness, busyness, noise, and distractions of the world that the immediate relief and comfort of God's presence is nearly impossible to describe in words.

4. SLOWING

Slowing for the purpose of godliness has been a significant spiritual discipline in my life that has also been a catalyst for the spiritual discipline of memorizing God's Word. In the Gospel of Mark, there is one particular verse that has been a great source of encouragement for slowing down the hurried pace of my life: "Then, because so many people were coming and going, they did not have a chance to eat, he said to them, 'Come with me by yourselves to a quiet place and get some rest'" (Mark 6:31).

In my personal life, I often find myself at the mercy of other people's agendas, schedules, and demands. Similar to the experience of Jesus Christ's disciples, I am in the company of people who are "coming and going," and I do not have a "chance to eat." The type of nourishment that I often lack when at the mercy of busyness, however, is not *physical* nourishment, but the *spiritual* nourishment that can only be provided by the Word of God.

Therefore, the spiritual discipline of slowing down to disengage the hurried pace of living has provided me with the much-needed time and space to experience greater awareness of God's presence.

I am convinced that the act of slowing is a much-needed spiritual discipline in my life and in the lives of the athletes I train and mentor. I reached this conclusion the first afternoon I decided to skip the drive and walk to the fitness studio I own and teach at in Santa Cruz.

Combining the spiritual disciplines of silence with the memorization of God's Word, I left my home, repeating Psalm 23 in my mind. Walking at a comfortable pace, I was amazed at how beautiful the route from my home to the studio was. Although I had driven it hundreds of times, it was not until I traveled on foot that I was able to fully behold the beauty of God's creation just steps from my doorway. In addition, there was something sacred about walking while repeating God's Word in my mind and I subsequently discovered that my ability to memorize and retain Bible verse was greatly increased when I engaged in moderate physical activity.

5. MEMORIZING GOD'S WORD

In Joshua 1:8, there is an amazing connection between Bible intake and meditation on God's Word: "This Book of the Law (God's Word) shall not depart from your mouth but you shall meditate on it day and night, so that you may be careful to do according to all that is written in it."

I know that in order for the Holy Spirit to speak in and through me, I must first have the Word of God readily available within my mind. Memorizing and "storing up" the Word of God is the first line of defense against temptation and fear, ensuring that God's Word will saturate my thinking and conversation with other people.

Furthermore, Bible memorization ensures that the Holy Spirit can bring a vital spiritual truth into my awareness at critical moments throughout my day. Memorizing God's Word for the purpose of godliness allows me to confront temptation, challenge, and dangerous situations with "the sword of the Spirit, which is the Word of God" (Ephesians 6:17).

In practicing the spiritual discipline of memorizing Scripture, I have found great benefit in writing Bible verses on 3x5 index cards and carrying my "memory card" with me throughout the day. I have discovered that as my intake of God's Word increases and is committed to memory, I tend to "think by the means of God's Word" throughout the day. In any given moment when I stop to reflect on the quality of my thinking, I am often overjoyed to find that the predominant thought in my mind was a verse from Scripture.

6. JOURNALING

When the Old Testament prophet Jeremiah expressed to God the depth of his grief about the fall of Jerusalem in his Lamentations, he was doing something not so different from the modern-day athlete who types his or her feelings into a word processor file named, "Daily Journal."

I have found journaling for the purpose of godliness helps me critically examine the direction my life is moving and express in a tangible and recordable way the magnificent question, "Am I increasing in spiritual maturity and godliness?"

Journaling was a huge component of my early training with Coach and was a practice that I advocated in my book, *Firebreather Fitness* and in the CrossFit goal-setting application course I taught around the world for several years.

"Am I increasing in spiritual maturity?" is a question the magnitude of which can only be honestly answered through the power and grace of the Holy Spirit. I believe the Psalmist shared a similar sentiment when he wrote, "Search me, O God, and know my heart; test me and know my anxious thoughts" (Psalm 139:23).

While journaling, I am able to move my thoughts from "head to paper," then read and reflect upon what the Holy Spirit has revealed to me. One of the greatest benefits of journaling for the purpose of godliness is the record of my thoughts and feelings for future reference.

Recently, while praying for God's shepherding and guidance in life, I felt the Holy Spirit direct me to review a prayer journal I had kept while undergoing platoon leadership training in the US Army Officer Candidate School. I was amazed to read the progression of my recorded thoughts and feelings from July 2005 to July 2006 and to note how fear, anxiety, and near-depression became the joy, comfort, and peacefulness of God's embrace and presence in my life.

Without the benefit of the journal during that time in my life, I could have easily been consumed by worry instead of the promise of God's faithfulness. As a result, I am committed to weekly journaling (often, daily) in which I ask such self-examining questions as, "Am I growing in my love for God?" and "How am I increasing in wisdom, stature, and favor with God?"

7. SIMPLICITY

One of the more challenging spiritual disciplines I have been practicing is *simplicity* for the purpose of godliness. In addition to the encouragement of several of my mentors, I was greatly inspired during a conversation with Father Cuneo on the spiritual benefits of simplicity.[21] He explained that in the Desert Father tradition, when a novice entered the monastery, the abbot stripped away the majority of his worldly possessions. In addition, the abbot reduced the novice's schedule to the basics of prayer, meditation, mealtime, and cleaning the monastery, which forced the novice to experience the simplicity of life.

Father Cuneo explained that once the distractions of life had been removed, all that remained for the novice to focus on was God.

In my life, I have happily discovered the hidden purpose of simplicity is to order my heart and priorities towards the single purpose of honoring God, and to live my life free from conflicting, egotistical, self-serving motives and habits.

One of the challenges I've faced with regard to simplicity has been overcoming my tendency to seek material objects and my seemingly endless desire to have "more stuff." I am often amazed at how easily my mind jumps from one object of desire to another and the worldly emphasis on advertising only makes the pursuit of simplicity that much more difficult.

Therefore, in my spiritual practice of simplicity, I have decided to use the "sword of the Spirit, which is the Word of God" (Ephesians 6:17) to help me combat the tendency of my mind to pursue worldly treasure. For example, when I find myself thinking about materialistic acquisitions, I repeat in my mind the teaching of Jesus Christ to, "Seek first the Kingdom of God and His righteousness" (Matthew 6:33).

I have happily discovered that within just a few repetitions of this specific verse, the craving for the material object begins to fade into the background of my consciousness, while the presence of God becomes my immediate focal point.

8. PRAYER

I experienced a pivotal turning point in my spiritual maturity after reading Donald Whitney's book, *Spiritual Disciplines for the Christian Life*. Whitney's argument that prayer should "always be just to the side and ready to take the place of what you are concentrating on" was singlehandedly one of the most motivating sentences I have ever read. [22]

Based on Whitney's argument and the Apostle Paul's direction to "pray without ceasing" (1 Thessalonians 5:17), prayer for the purpose of godliness has become one of my most cherished spiritual disciplines and is one I strongly encourage to the athletes I train and mentor.

In the pursuit of modeling my life after Jesus Christ, I strive to follow his example of prayer seen throughout the four Gospels. For example, in the Gospel of Luke, I find inspiration in the account of Jesus "withdrawing to desolate places to pray" (Luke 5:16), as it demonstrates the synergistic benefit of combining the spiritual disciplines of solitude and prayer.

Modeling the example of Jesus, I have designated times of prayer set aside each day, which compliment my spiritual disciplines of silence, solitude, and the intake of God's Word. I have found great benefit in allowing the Holy Spirit to influence and guide my prayers through Scripture. I also follow the recommendation of D.A. Carson in his wonderful book, *Praying with Paul*, and try to model my prayers after the Apostle Paul. [23]

I have further discovered that combining the spiritual disciplines of Bible intake, prayer, and meditation together has helped "smooth out the rough edges" of my prayer life. Specifically, I have noted that when I begin reading from God's Word, then smoothly transition into a period of silent meditation on a particular verse from Scripture, then gradually allow God's Word to influence the direction of my prayers, the three disciplines seamlessly integrate together with a beauty hard to articulate in words.

This particular model of integrating God's Word with meditation and prayer was also expressed by the Psalmist when he wrote, "May the words of my mouth [God's Word] and the meditation of my heart [meditation] be acceptable [prayer] in your sight, O Lord, my rock and my redeemer" (Psalm 19:14).[24]

A WARRIOR TRADITION STORY ON THE POWER OF PRAYER

During the first Gulf War, a young Marine Corps lieutenant received word that his platoon would advance across the desert at daybreak. This was a task he was prepared for yet feared. There was absolutely no cover or concealment across the vast open desert. His platoon would be visible to the enemy and an easy target for a machine gun.

That night, the lieutenant lay awake and prayed, "Please God, keep my men safe. Watch over my men. If anyone must fall in tomorrow's battle, let it be me."

Suddenly, the usual starry and clear night became overcast and a light rain started to fall on the dry desert floor. The light rain became a steady downpour to the amazement of the marines on the ground. This was the first time their platoon had encountered anything but heat and aridity.

The lieutenant radioed other platoons along the border to inquire about their conditions. "Is anyone else getting poured on?" he asked.

"All clear and dry in our sector," reported other officers.

The lieutenant was astonished and took the rain as a sign that his platoon was doomed. He wondered, "Why, God, would you rain on my men the night before our battle?"

In the morning, the sun returned and the desert sand quickly dried. As the young marines prepared to advance across the border onto the vast and open desert, they noticed what appeared to be glistening discs along the surface of the sand. The torrential rain had uncovered and exposed an Iraqi minefield. Had the rain not fallen, the platoon would have walked right into an enemy kill zone.

The grateful lieutenant, his prayer answered, returned to God in prayer, saying, "Thank you, God, for keeping my men safe."

FINDING WHAT WORKS

Spiritual disciplines encourage us to "press toward the goal for the prize of the upward call of God in Christ Jesus" (Philippians 3:13-14). They involve deliberate and intentional training and practice, with the specific purpose of increasing in godliness.

One consistent attribute of great professional athletes I have mentored (in addition to successful business executives and CEOs) is the amount of time they spent each day in mastering their pursuit, whether it's sport or business. In the same manner, the amount of time spent within the practice of spiritual disciplines is of immense importance. As with any relationship, I have discovered that the best way for me to gain increased intimacy with God is to spend time with Him.

My recommendation to you is this: based on the eight spiritual disciplines I have outlined, pick one or two disciplines that resonate with your heart and commit yourself to them for the next nine weeks of training. Keep in mind that these spiritual disciplines would potentially be in addition to the daily period of meditation and breathwork that we've already covered.

The spiritual disciplines are meant to provide you with a means to experience the presence of God in your life. Therefore, even a few minutes each day of *quality* time in the disciplines will have an immensely positive effect in every area of your life.

It's my prayer for you that the Holy Spirit reveal the spiritual disciplines that provide the greatest "increase in wisdom, stature, and favor with God and mankind" (Luke 2:52) and support your intention for success, happiness, and true fulfillment in life.

A WARRIOR TRADITION STORY ON THE POWER OF INFLUENCE

One morning, a young man was walking along the seashore after a horrific storm. The beach was strewn with seaweed, driftwood, and debris. He thought to himself, "This has been such a terrible and powerful storm."

As he continued walking, he noticed far in the distance an old man, who despite his age, seemed to be dancing along the shore. Getting closer, he saw the old man was picking up starfish from the sand and throwing them back into the ocean.

"What are you doing," he asked.

The old man replied, "The sun is going to come up soon and the tide is going out. If I don't throw these starfish back into the ocean, they are going to die."

"Silly old man, you can't possibly make a difference," the young man said. "There are thousands of starfish washed up on the beach."

A knowing smile flashed across the old man's face as he bent down and picked up another starfish, which he hurled far out into the sea. "Well, sonny, it made a difference to that one."

And with those words, the old man continued in his efforts to save the lives of the starfish, one at a time. The young man, greatly moved and influenced by the old man, joined him in the effort.

Then, a woman appeared in the distance, walking toward them and no doubt wondering why they were dancing on the shore.

What influence do we have? Are we able to change the tides of our lives and direct the currents in the lives of others? The Warriors Code dictates that we are responsible—despite the odds stacked against us—to serve and support others. The warrior believes every life is worth saving; the warrior knows his or her influence can start universal momentum that has the power to change the world.

— SPIRITUAL DISCIPLINE TRAINING JOURNAL —

CHOOSE TWO OR MORE SPIRITUAL DISCIPLINES EACH WEEK FOR THE NEXT 9-WEEKS AND RECORD YOUR REFLECTIONS.

LIFE CHANGING RESULTS AWAIT WHEN YOU INTEGRATE:

1) PROPER PHYSICAL NUTRITION

2) HEALTHY MENTAL NUTRITION

3) THE EIGHT SPIRITUAL DISCIPLINES

4) CHALLENGING PHYSICAL TRAINING

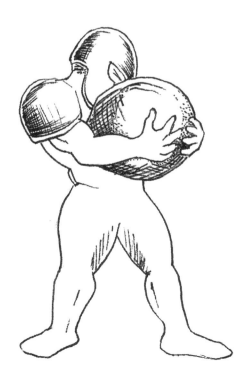

SPIRITUAL DISCIPLINES WEEK #1:

❏ Solitude / Silence

❏ Meditation

❏ Slowing

❏ Memorizing God's Word

❏ Journaling

❏ Simplicity

❏ Prayer

❏ Forgiveness

JOURNAL REFLECTIONS:

SPIRITUAL DISCIPLINES WEEK #2:

❏ **Solitude / Silence**

❏ **Meditation**

❏ **Slowing**

❏ **Memorizing God's Word**

❏ **Journaling**

❏ **Simplicity**

❏ **Prayer**

❏ **Forgiveness**

JOURNAL REFLECTIONS:

SPIRITUAL DISCIPLINES WEEK #3:

❏ Solitude / Silence

❏ Meditation

❏ Slowing

❏ Memorizing God's Word

❏ Journaling

❏ Simplicity

❏ Prayer

❏ Forgiveness

JOURNAL REFLECTIONS:

SPIRITUAL DISCIPLINES WEEK #4:

❏ **Solitude / Silence**

❏ **Meditation**

❏ **Slowing**

❏ **Memorizing God's Word**

❏ **Journaling**

❏ **Simplicity**

❏ **Prayer**

❏ **Forgiveness**

JOURNAL REFLECTIONS:

SPIRITUAL DISCIPLINES WEEK #5:

❏ Solitude / Silence

❏ Meditation

❏ Slowing

❏ Memorizing God's Word

❏ Journaling

❏ Simplicity

❏ Prayer

❏ Forgiveness

JOURNAL REFLECTIONS:

SPIRITUAL DISCIPLINES WEEK #6:

❏ **Solitude / Silence**

❏ **Meditation**

❏ **Slowing**

❏ **Memorizing God's Word**

❏ **Journaling**

❏ **Simplicity**

❏ **Prayer**

❏ **Forgiveness**

JOURNAL REFLECTIONS:

SPIRITUAL DISCIPLINES WEEK #7:

❏ Solitude / Silence

❏ Meditation

❏ Slowing

❏ Memorizing God's Word

❏ Journaling

❏ Simplicity

❏ Prayer

❏ Forgiveness

JOURNAL REFLECTIONS:

SPIRITUAL DISCIPLINES WEEK #8:

❏ Solitude / Silence

❏ Meditation

❏ Slowing

❏ Memorizing God's Word

❏ Journaling

❏ Simplicity

❏ Prayer

❏ Forgiveness

JOURNAL REFLECTIONS:

SPIRITUAL DISCIPLINES WEEK #9:

❑ Solitude / Silence

❑ Meditation

❑ Slowing

❑ Memorizing God's Word

❑ Journaling

❑ Simplicity

❑ Prayer

❑ Forgiveness

JOURNAL REFLECTIONS:

PART THREE
THE BODY

PART THREE: THE BODY

NUTRITION

It all begins with nutrition.

For the athletes I train at CrossFit Amundson and to you, the reader, I recommend a specific nutritional plan that I cited earlier, in the *Mental Nutrition* section: Dr. Barry Sears' Zone Diet, which he debuted in his first book, *Enter The Zone*. My contention is that integrated training should be more than just an elite fitness and conditioning program: living the victorious philosophy is a way of life.

The lessons learned in the gym are directly applicable to life outside the gym, including the kitchen. Therefore, I find it perfectly logical that the word "diet" comes from a Greek root meaning "way of life" and that eating in the "Zone" is a way of life that supports a healthy body and mind.

The "Zone" is Dr. Sears' term for proper hormonal balance and he claims that a 40:30:30 calorie ratio of low-glycemic carbs (mostly fruits and veggies) to low-fat protein has several great effects on the body, the first being that this ratio of nutrients prompts the release of moderate amounts of the hormones insulin and glycogen, which together trigger the release of a flood of feel-good chemicals called eicosanoids. These chemicals help protect your heart, open the bronchi of the lungs, and reduce inflammation.

A secondary effect of significance to athletes is this ratio also leads to fat loss, increased muscle mass, and increased athletic capacity.

In addition to the ratio, the other main aspect of the Zone Diet is portion control. Athletes are allotted a certain number of "blocks" of food a day for their size and exercise level. A block, in the Zone system, is defined as a balanced unit of food, composed of the following three sub-blocks: protein (seven grams, i.e., one ounce of chicken, one egg, 1.5 ounces of fish); carbs (nine grams, i.e., half an apple, four cups of broccoli, one cup strawberries); and fat (1.5 grams, i.e., three olives, three almonds, one teaspoon of olive oil.).

According to the Zone, "average" men and women need fourteen and eleven blocks per day, respectively, and a six-foot-tall, one-hundred eighty-five-pound man would require sixteen to eighteen blocks a day. In the *Victory* plan, I encourage you to consume lean and fresh protein sources and eat only fruits and veggies as a carbohydrate source.

UNDERSTANDING ZONE BLOCKS

A "Zone Block" is a measurement unit used to simplify the process of making balanced meals:
- Seven grams of protein = one block of protein
- Nine grams of carbohydrate = one block of carbohydrate
- 1.5 grams of fat = one block of fat (we assume there is already about 1.5 grams of fat in each block of protein, so the total amount of fat needed per one block meal is three grams)

When a meal is composed of equal blocks of protein, carbohydrate, and fat, it is 40 percent carbohydrate, 30 percent protein and 30 percent fat.

On the next page are my recommended foods, their macronutrient category (protein, carbohydrate, or fat), along with a conversion of measurements to blocks.

To make a Zone meal, simply choose one item from the protein list, one item from the carbohydrate list, and one item from the fat list to compose a one-block meal. Or choose two items from each column to compose a two-block meal, etc.

DETERMINING YOUR IDEAL BLOCK COUNT

I have been following the Zone Diet for nearly twenty years and the benefits continue to astound me. This diet works and it's easy to follow. To determine your ideal daily total block allotment, simply consult the chart.

Choose your body type to determine your daily block allotment.						
BREAKFAST	LUNCH	SNACK	DINNER	SNACK	TOTAL DAILY BLOCKS	BODY TYPE
2	2	2	2	2	10	Small Female
3	3	1	3	1	11	Medium Female
3	3	2	3	2	14	Large Female
4	4	1	4	1	14	Athletic - Well Muscled Female
4	4	2	4	2	16	Small Male
5	5	1	5	1	17	Medium Male
5	5	2	5	2	19	Large Male
4	4	4	4	4	20	X-Large Male
5	5	3	5	4	22	XXL Male
5	5	5	5	5	25	Athletic - Well Muscled Male

ZONE BLOCK GUIDELINES

ZONE BLOCK ALLOTMENTS FOR PROTEIN, FAT & CARBOHYDRATE

PROTEIN (COOKED QUANTITY)	
beef	1 oz
calamari	1 1/2 oz
canadian bacon	1 oz
canned tuna	1 oz
catfish	1 1/2 oz
cheese	1 oz
chicken breast	1 oz
clams	1 1/2 oz
corned beef	1 oz
cottage cheese	1/4 cup
crabmeat	1 1/2 oz
duck	1 1/2 oz
egg substitute	1/4 cup
egg whites	2 large
egg (whole)	1 large
feta cheese	1 1/2 oz
flounder/sole	1 1/2 oz
ground beef	1 1/2 oz
ground lamb	1 1/2 oz
ground pork	1 1/2 oz
ground turkey	1 1/2 oz
ham	1 oz
lamb	1 oz
lobster	1 1/2 oz
pork	1 oz
protein powder	1 oz
ricotta cheese	2 oz
salmon	1 1/2 oz
sardines	1 oz
scallops	1 1/2 oz
seitan	1 oz
shrimp	1 1/2 oz
soy burgers	1/2 patty
soy cheese	1 oz
soy sausage	2 links
spirulina (dried)	1/2 oz
swordfish	1 1/2 oz
tofu (firm)	2 oz
tofu (soft)	3 oz
tuna steak	1 1/2 oz
turkey breast	1 oz
veal	1 oz

CARBOHYDRATE (COOKED)	
artichoke	1 small
asparagus	12 spears
beet greens	1 1/4 cup
black beans	1/4 cup
bok choy	3 cups
broccoli	1 1/4 cup
brussel sprouts	3/4 cup
cabbage	1 1/3 cup
cauliflower	1 1/4 cup
chick peas	1/4 cup
collard greens	1 1/4 cup
dill pickles	3 (3 in)
eggplant	1 1/2 cup
fava beans	1/3 cup
green beans	1 cup

CARBOHYDRATE (RAW)	
alfalfa sprouts	7 1/2 cup
apple	1/2
apple sauce	3/8 cup
apricots	3 small
bean sprouts	3 cups
blackberries	1/2 cup
blueberries	1/2 cup
broccoli	2 cups
cantaloupe	1/4
cabbage	2 1/4 cups
cauliflower	2 cups
celery	2 cups
cherries	7
cucumber	1 (9 in)
fruit cocktail	1/3 cup
grapefruit	1/2
grapes	1/2 cup
honeydew	1/2
kiwi	1
lemon	1
lettuce, Iceburg	1 head
lettuce, romaine	6 cups
lime	1
mushrooms	3 cups
nectarine	1/2

CARBOHYDRATE (COOKED)	
kale	1 1/4 cup
kidney beans	1/4 cup
leeks	1 cup
lentils	1/4 cup
oatmeal	1/3 cup
okra	3/4 cup
onions	1/2 cup
saurkraut	1 cup
spagetti squash	1 cup
spinach	1 1/3 cup
swiss chard	1 1/4 cup
tomato sauce	1/2 cup
tomatoes	3/4 cup
yellow squash	1 1/4 cup
zuccini	1 1/3 cup

CARBOHYDRATE (RAW)	
onion	2/3 cup
orange	1/2
peach	1
pear	1/2
peppers	1 1/4 cup
pinapple	1/2 cup
plum	1
radishes	2 cups
raspberries	2/3 cup
salsa	1/2 cup
snow peas	3/4 cup
spinach	4 cups
strawberries	1 cup
tangerine	1
tomato	1 cup
watermelon	2/4 cup

COMBO ITEMS (QUANTITY)	
milk	1 cup
soybeans	1/4 cup
soymilk	1 cup
tempeh	1 1/2 cup
yogurt (plain)	1/2 cup

FAT (QUANTITY)	
Almonds	~3
Avocado	1 Tbs
bacon bits	2 1/2 tsp
butter	1/3 tsp
canola oil	1/3 tsp
cashews	~3
cream cheese	1 tsp
cream, light	1/2 tsp
guacamole	1/2 Tbs
half and half	1 Tbs
lard	1/3 tsp
macadamia nuts	~1
mayo, light	1 tsp
mayonnaise	1/3 tsp
olive oil	1/3 tsp
olives	~5
peanut butter	1/2 tsp
peanut oil	1/3 tsp
peanuts	~6
seseme oil	1/3 tsp
sour cream	1 tsp
sunflower seeds	1/4 tsp
tahini	1/3 tsp
tartar sauce	1/2 tsp
veg. shortening	1/3 tsp
vegetable oil	1/3 tsp

*NOTE: Combo items contain 1 block of protein and 1 block of carbohydrate.

ZONE BLOCK ALLOTMENTS FOR UNFAVORABLE CARBOHYDRATES

CARBOHYDRATE (QUANTITY)	
VEGETABLES	
Acorn Squash	3/8 cup
Baked Beans	1/8 cup
Beets	1/2 cup
Black-eyed peas	1/4 cup
Butternut Squash	1/3 cup
Cooked carrots	1/2 cup
Corn	1/4 cup
French Fries	5
Hubbard squash	2/3 cup
Lima beans	1/4 cup
Parsnips	1/3 (9 in)
Peas	1/3 cup
Pinto Beans	1/4 cup
Potato, boiled	1/3 cup
Potato, mashed	1/5 cup
Refried beans	1/4 cup
Sweet Potato, baked	1/3 (5 in)
Sweet potato, mashed	1/5 cup
Turnip	3/4 cup
FRUIT	
Banana	1/3 (9 in)
Cranberries	1/4 cup
Cranberry sauce	4 tsp
Dates	2
Figs	3/4
Guava	1/2 cup
Kumquat	3
Mango	1/3 cup
Papaya	2/3 cup
Prunes	2
Raisins	1 Tbs
FRUIT JUICE	
Apple juice	1/3 cup
Cranberry juice	1/4 cup
Fruit Punch	1/4 cup
Grape juice	1/4 cup
Grapefruit juice	3/8 cup
Lemon juice	1/3 cup
Orange juice	3/8 cup
Pineapple juice	1/4 cup
Tomato juice	3/4 cup

CARBOHYDRATE (QUANTITY)	
VEGETABLES	
Bagel	1/4
Barley	1 Tbs
Biscuit	1/4
Baked Potato	1/3 cup
Bread	1/2 slice
Bread crumbs	1/2 oz
Breadstick	1
Buckwheat	1/2 oz
Bulgur wheat	1/2 oz
Cereal	1/2 oz
Corn bread	1 in square
Cornstarch	4 tsp
Croissant	1/4
Crouton	1/2 oz
Donut	1/4
English muffin	1/4
Flour	1 1/2 tsp
Granola	1/2 oz
Grits	1/3 cup
Melba toast	1/2 oz
Muffins	1/4
Noodles	1/4 cup
Oatmeal (Instant)	1/2 packet
Pasta, Cooked	1/4 cup
Pasta, high protein	1/3 cup
Pancake	1/2 (4 in)
Pita bread	1/4
Popcorn	2 cups
Rice	3 Tbs
Rice cake	1
Roll (hamburger, hot dog)	1/4
Roll (dinner)	1/2
Taco shell	1
Tortilla (corn)	1 (6 in)
Tortilla (flour)	1/2 (6 in)
Udon noodles	3 Tbs
Waffle	1/2

CARBOHYDRATE (QUANTITY)	
CONDIMENTS	
BBQ sauce	2 Tbs
Brown sugar	1 1/2 tsp
Cocktail sauce	2 Tbs
Confectioners sugar	1 Tbs
Granulated sugar	2 tsp
Honey	1/2 Tbs
Jelly/jam	2 tsp
Ketchup	2 Tbs
Maple syrup	2 tsp
Molasses	2 tsp
Pickle (bread and butter)	6 slices
Plum sauce	1 1/2 Tbs
Relish (sweet)	4 tsp
Steak sauce	2 Tbs
Teriyaki sauce	1 1/2 Tbs

ALCOHOL	
Beer	8 oz
Liquor	1 oz
Wine	4 oz

SNACKS	
Chocolate bar	1/2 oz
Corn chips	1/2 oz
Graham crackers	1 1/2
Ice cream	1/4 cup
Potato chips	1/2 cup
Pretzels	1/2 oz
Saltine crackers	4
Tortilla chips	1/2 oz

*NOTE: When building meals
with "unfavorable carbohydrates"
quantity becomes critical.

———— SAMPLE MEAL PLANS ————

SAMPLE DAILY MEAL PLAN: 16-BLOCK

Consult your block allotment and adjust accordingly. These are some of my favorite meals. After nearly two decades of Zone nutrition, I've concluded that simplicity is the key to sustainability.

BREAKFAST (3 BLOCKS)
- 3 Hard-boiled eggs (3 blocks protein)
- 3 Sliced kiwi (3 blocks carb)
- 9 Almonds (3 blocks fat)

SNACK (2 BLOCKS)
- ½ Cup low-fat cottage cheese (2 blocks protein)
- 1 Cup sliced strawberries (1 block carb)
- ½ Cup blueberries (1 block carb)
- 1 tsp. Crushed walnuts (2 blocks fat)

LUNCH (4 BLOCKS)
- 4 oz. Sliced chicken breast (4 blocks protein)
- Large salad with sun-dried tomatoes and other veggies (3 blocks carb)
- 1 Fuji apple sliced into salad (1 block carb)
- Extra-virgin olive oil & balsamic dressing (4 blocks fat)

SNACK (3 BLOCKS)
- 2 Scoops protein powder (21 grams/3 blocks protein)
- 1 Banana (3 blocks carb)
- 1 Scoop peanut butter (3 blocks fat)
- Mix with water to taste

DINNER (4 BLOCKS)
- 3 Scrambled eggs (3 blocks protein)
- 1 oz. Chicken scrambled into eggs (1 block protein)
- 2 Wheat tortilla (4 blocks carb)
- 4 tbsp. Avocado (4 blocks fat)

THE SEVEN-DAY PHYSICAL AND MENTAL CHALLENGE

Are you up for a life-changing challenge? This exercise is a practice in awareness and empowering yourself to make conscious choices. For the next seven days, eat Zone-proportioned meals with only desirable macronutrient food choices. Consciously choose to consume fruits and vegetables as your carbohydrates, lean meats and fish as your protein choices, and monounsaturated fats as your fat choice.

Beverage choices are water, tea, or coffee. No sugar may be added to the beverages, and extra cream, milk, or half-and-half all "count" and must be factored into total allotment of daily food intake.

My recommendation is to prepare your meals in the morning and pack them in Tupperware for the day. Make sure you consume your allotted daily food intake—nothing more and nothing less.

Be very disciplined: it's only for seven days, so give 110-percent effort. If you have an undesirable meal, snack or piece of food, you must return to the beginning of the seven-day challenge.

At the same time you are making conscious choices about the physical nutrition of your day, pay special attention to your mental nutrition as well. Only consume positive words, mantras, and affirmations during the seven-day challenge. You may feel a tendency to briefly entertain a negative word or thought pattern. If this happens, first take a moment and congratulate yourself for having awareness of your thoughts. Next, immediately stop the pattern and substitute a positive word or statement for the negative one.

Here is how this might play out:

Statement: *"I keep getting hurt."*

Three seconds later, the thought: *"Whoa! I don't really mean that!"*

Then replace the negative statement with: *"I am resilient and healthy."*

If you were able to quickly replace the negative with the positive, continue onward with the seven-day challenge. These moments will come less and less, and you will become more and more conscious of the thoughts and words you entertain and vocalize.

If, on the other hand, after you verbalize or entertain any negative thoughts and continue down that dark road with thoughts or words like, "I must not be a good athlete" or "My luck is always down" or "Everyone is stronger than me," you must go back to the beginning of the seven-day challenge.

Final rule: *the physical and mental challenges run simultaneously; if you restart in one, you must restart in the other.*

AN EMPOWERING CONSIDERATION

When I started my CrossFit training, neither the CrossFit Games nor the sport of fitness had been fully developed. I felt no rush to achieve elite athletic capacity overnight and embraced the idea that the purpose of physical training was to achieve and maintain fitness over a lifetime. Therefore, I took a "longevity" approach to my training and understood that on my journey as an athlete and coach, I had a lifetime of learning opportunities. This approach relieved a lot of pressure and helped me learn to enjoy the process of my development rather than any specific outcome.

In my travels as a coach and during conversations with athletes at the CrossFit goal-setting trainer course, one of the themes I hear is a sense of urgency to achieve overnight success and dominance in CrossFit (or business, relationships, school, etc.). This self-imposed and completely illusory time limit may actually hinder development and take away from the simple joy of the moments we spend in the gym.

Coach told me the day I started CrossFit that I would see ten years of adaptation. My training journal is a testament to the wisdom and truth of his statement. After nearly twenty years in CrossFit, I continue to refine my nutritional intake, improve my metabolic conditioning, and enhance my gymnastic and weightlifting technique and ability, and I continue to set personal records in the gym along the way.

Most importantly of all, my love for the expression of fitness in sport or any other endeavor both inside and outside the gym remains constant. I believe that when you embrace an integrated approach to training, while simultaneously eating both good "physical" and "mental" nutrition, you can achieve and maintain amazing levels of fitness for your entire life.

LEGEND OF THE FIREBREATHER!

There were six of us sprawled across the floor after performing a timed workout comprised of two movements: a thruster (a blend of front squats and push presses) and a pull-up. On the whiteboard that morning, it didn't stand out in any way. But this thruster-pull-up workout (later named "Fran" by CrossFit founder Coach Greg Glassman; 21,15,9 repetitions of barbell thruster and pull-up) had pushed us into the redline territory of extreme physical exertion and banging into and over the anaerobic threshold. It was a scorcher of a workout, literally and figuratively, as each of us looked at one another and noticed how our throats had been seared by the breathing and metabolic intensity that comes with an all-out effort.

"It felt like I was breathing fire the entire time!" I proclaimed in a raspy voice. "It's like we're a bunch of firebreathers!"

That word stuck, and the word "firebreather" quickly became a term of endearment, compliment, and "status" within the gym. For years the term was used to qualify and quantify an athlete who had achieved a certain level of physical capacity within the gym. However, in my travels teaching CrossFit around the world, I soon realized that being a firebreather has much more to do with the intangible realm of capacity, and is best recognized in an athlete who brings all of their energy, spirit and intent to training—with a burning purpose to give it their absolute best.

Based on the requests of thousands of athletes, in early 2008 I decided to officially define the term Firebreather with a two-part definition:

1. **One who faces the trials and tribulations of great physical opposition with an indomitable spirit.**
   To be a Firebreather, you take on this opposition by training as if your life depends on it. When you make that kind of commitment, incredible amounts of energy and ability will be realized. I faced opposition in my jobs in law enforcement and military service. But opposition can also refer to the trials and tribulations that come with taking on any significant goal.

2. **An Optimistic energy associated with the heart of the athlete.**

The "heart of an athlete" is key. Think about approaching your workouts and your life as a professional athlete. Even if you have only an hour (or less) to invest in your physical, mental, and spiritual training each day, approach it with the energy and focus of an Olympic athlete. Pour your heart into your training, focus on the effort you put into each workout, and the results will astonish you.

—— AND NOW ... IT'S TIME TO WORKOUT! ——

UNDERSTANDING THE 21 DAY PLANS

The 21-Day training plans are designed to incrementally develop your confidence, technique, and capacity in a combined weightlifting and gymnastic conditioning program, and to introduce you to the concepts of an integrated and holistic approach to fitness. These workouts have been "battle proven" by myself, hundreds of athletes from my gym in Santa Cruz, CA., and thousands of people who have read my book, *Firebreather Fitness*. Simply put – these workouts will WORK for you! For exercise descriptions, I recommend visiting the "Firebreather Fitness" playlist on my YouTube channel at YouTube.com/AmundsonGreg. I am making more emphasis in the following 9-week plan on your nutrition than I did in my book. Every fourth day, you will take an "active rest day" and will also take time to prepare your meals for the following three days of training.

Note that many of the weightlifting skills take place *after* your gymnastic conditioning. This is crucial to the philosophy for optimal integrated fitness, which involves maintaining strength at a high heart rate. Just ask any military operator or law-enforcement officer, and he or she will confirm that in critical moments when you need your strength, you will need it at a high heart rate. Your training should reflect and prepare you for the demands of life!

Also, note that rather than prescribing a specific weight to utilize on the barbell skills, you are training at a percentage of your relative strength. This specific percentage, unique within the training cycle you are in, will be assigned in the workouts.

The plan includes your physical workouts along with a basic set of rituals to weave into your day: first words, meditation, box breathing, and positive affirmations.

If you are new to these movements and practices, you may at first feel overwhelmed or a little intimidated. The key is to take the next 9-weeks one workout at a time. The program I have designed for you offers an excellent opportunity to practice the power of micro-goals. Commit to the macro-goal of completing the big 9-week plan, and then narrow your focus to the task list for Day One. Make that your universe! This way, all you have to focus on is completing a small set of tasks during the course of a single day. The discipline to take life one moment at a time, and to remain aware and committed to living in the present, is the *Victory* way and skill of a warrior. Therefore, take these workouts and spiritual practices one day at a time, trusting in the compound effect and long-term benefit the program will provide.

UNDERSTANDING THE VICTORY PROGRAM

I created the physical component of the *Victory* training program with the intention of making your workouts simple, sustainable, effective, efficient, and fun!

Limited time in the day is a given for most of us. In military and law-enforcement work, there is no such thing as an eight-hour workday, and the same can be said for so many professions—doctors, teachers, executives, parents. There are already myriad responsibilities demanding your time and energy. You want and need a high-performance training plan that can be easily incorporated into your everyday routine.

Because this program is made of up high-intensity workouts, most of your workouts will range between 8 and 20 minutes in duration, and only rarely will they take longer than 30 minutes. Believe me when I say that 8 minutes of high-intensity exercise is far more effective than an hour of bopping around a gym doing a few sets of bench presses here and there. When you work out this way, it frees up more energy and productivity for your daily life. You will see the difference for yourself in a matter of weeks.

The *Victory* program makes use of basic gym equipment. For years, the fitness world gravitated toward expensive weight machines, like Nautilus and Cybex. These machines were designed to isolate individual muscles. The technology to deliver this concept grew ever more expensive and complicated in motorized resistance machines with embedded computers.

I've seen and tried a variety of fitness programs, and I can say with confidence: Basic equipment produces better results. A pull-up bar or set of gymnastics rings is far more effective than an expensive cable-crossover machine. Yes, you read that correctly: The bar at the local playground is more valuable to you as a Firebreather than the machines crowded into a conventional gym. There are a number of basic gymnastics movements requiring nothing more than bodyweight for resistance that will get you into phenomenal physical condition. Don't underestimate the power of these exercises.

This program also incorporates weights in classic lifts like bench press, squats, and thrusters. It's the combination of functional movements, both the bodyweight exercises and those where you are working against heavy resistance, done at high intensity—that will make you a champion in every area of your life.

If a home gym isn't possible for you, then get creative! You could, for example, keep a mobile gym in your car. Pack rings, dumbbells, kettlebells, jump rope, and a medicine ball, and find a park to work out in. I know several athletes who take this approach, driving to a variety of outdoor locations throughout the week to work out. At my gym in Santa Cruz, I have a 12-passenger van that I load up with gear, and take members to the beach or hills to work out. When you develop the "eye of a Firebreather" the world becomes your gym!

If you have access to a gym with free weights and a pull-up bar, you can do the program. You may need to innovate at times to do the workouts. If, for example, a workout calls for running, thrusters, and pull-ups, then you might have to figure out a plan where you can use a barbell or dumbbells for the thrusters near a pull-up bar so that you prevent others from taking over a piece of equipment in the middle of your session. If it's impossible to run outside or jump on a treadmill for the runs, then you can substitute in a similar activity, like rowing, or something as simple as air squats.

TO BE SUCCESSFUL, EVERY WORKOUT MUST FOCUS ON ACHIEVING THESE THREE THINGS:

1. **GOOD TECHNIQUE.** Learning how to do the movements properly is not an overnight process. Practice and perfect them. Technique also includes range of motion, which naturally lends itself to the next point, intensity. I recommend training under the care of a well qualified CrossFit coach. In addition, my book *Firebreather Fitness* is a great resource for proper mechanics and technique training in the exercises that follow in the *Victory* program.

2. **HIGH INTENSITY.** With good technique intact, maintaining a high level of intensity and effort will pay off, delivering metabolic stimulus and adaptation. Every workout is set up with time as a critical component. You are either doing as much work as you can in a given time, or completing a piece of work in the least amount of time possible. The principle I teach Law Enforcement officers when they train is applicable to everyone: "When you workout, train as if your life depends in it – because it does!"

3. **CONSISTENCY.** Schedule workouts in such a way that there is no danger of them being trumped by other things. Early mornings are a good time for many people, before others are awake and start making demands on their time. Get it done! It's a great way to start the day. If early mornings aren't an option for you, then commit to working out at a specific time of day.

Consistent, high-intensity efforts using functional movements and proper technique are the secret to long-term, steady progress.

Most fitness programs fall short because they don't offer the level of precision and personalization that you would get from a coach. Rather than a having, for example, a shirt tailored just for you, it's more like one size fits most: the results will be mixed. My mission is to give you a set of tools to drive you rapidly toward a state of highly tuned physical fitness. These tools allow you to customize the training program to your current state of fitness. In addition, as your get stronger, the workouts will "get stronger" right along side you. In other words, you will never outgrow the program!

UNDERSTANDING THRESHOLD TRAINING

Many people preparing to do a workout have a problem: figuring out how much to do and how hard to go. *Victory* threshold training is designed to take the guesswork out of determining that load. A short test before key workouts will let you know exactly what your training intensity (reps or weight) should be for each movement.

Mash-up tests will help you find out how many reps you can do of a specific movement in one minute. Each test includes two or three movements.

UNDERSTANDING 1-REP MAX TESTS

1-REP MAX TESTS

For the strength-specific components in the plans, you will need to find your 1-rep max for different movements. So when the program instructs you to "find your 1-rep max deadlift," you will work toward the most you can lift with the given movement in a safe, controlled, and skilled manner. Knowing what a 1-rep max is for a certain weight movement will allow you to work on that movement with more reps, using specific percentages of your max.

Consider the thruster. On Day 3, you'll start your workout by figuring out what your 1-rep max is with thrusters. At the end the test, you will see this set:

5 THRUSTERS (60% 1RM)

If your 1-rep max on the thruster was 100 pounds, the last task of Day 3 would be to perform 5 high-quality thrusters with 60 pounds.

UNDERSTANDING THE MASH-UP TEST

Both a workout and also a time trial, the Mash Up Test is a way to get real-time info on where your fitness stands so you can both chart your overall progress as well as dial in the optimal workout load and intensity for the day.

To explain, let's take a look at a basic mash-up test: jump-rope double unders and kettlebell swings. You will do a one-minute test of each movement to get an accurate data point on your fitness and skills.

1. First, count the number of double unders you can do in one minute. Start the clock and do as many as you can before that minute is up. Beginner athletes can do traditional single jumps.
2. Record the total number of repetitions completed in a journal or on the whiteboard. Rest 1 minute to recover.
3. Next, see how many kettlebell swings you can do in 1 minute. Record the number of reps completed.
4. Rest 2 minutes to recover.

What's next?

Following your 2-minute recovery, determine the threshold percentage to use in the workout. During the initial stages of the 21-day *Victory* Program you will be training at 40 percent of your maximum capacity achieved on the 1-minute test.

For example, let's say you did 100 double unders and 30 kettlebell swings in the mash-up. Multiply these numbers by 40 percent, or 0.4, each. You get:

- 40 double unders
- 12 kettlebell swings

Plug these numbers into the 7-round workout of the day, which totals 14 minutes. At the start of minute one, you do 40 double unders. Rest the remainder of the minute until minute 2 begins, then start your first set of 12 kettlebell swings. After the 12 swings, put down the kettlebell, pick up the rope, and wait until minute 3 begins to start the next set of double under repetitions.

Every odd minute you're on the jump rope, and every even minute you're swinging the kettlebell. The 14-minute workout is written like this:

- Every Minute on the Minute (or EMOM for short) for 14:00 (7 rounds of each)
- Odd minutes = 40% threshold for jump rope
- Even minutes = 40% threshold for kettlebell swing

A PROGRESSIVE PROGRAM

Within each week, the program will offer workouts where the percentage increases to bring the athlete closer to the threshold. This promotes adaptation.

The mash-up and 1-rep max tests make the program more flexible. As strength and fitness grows, the reps/weight will increase.

As mentioned, the plans also include standard baseline workouts, strength-specific components, and Fitness Outside the Box activities.

TAKE IT OUTSIDE

One rut I want you to avoid is doing all of your training inside a gym. I feel so strongly about this that I have designed the *Victory* programs with it in mind. Built into the 21-day training plans are assigned workouts that say: "Fitness Outside the Box."

Getting outside has innumerable health benefits. Perhaps the most vital health benefit from being outside is adequate sun exposure. Many Americans suffer from a deficiency in vitamin D—also known as "the sunshine vitamin." Some three-quarters of Americans are reported to be deficient in this nutrient. Scientists are beginning to connect the dots between the risk of heart disease and cancer when it comes to a lack of the sunshine vitamin, as well as linking low vitamin D intake to bone-density loss and rickets.

Less tangible health connections to taking your workouts to the back yard, a beach, or a local park include the dimensions of spiritual and mental health. Being outside is just plain fun. Doing all of your training inside a gym can be a drag on you. Fresh air, sunshine, new places to be and train— all of this is psychologically restorative and spiritually powerful. Get on a bike, hike up a trail, go for a swim, find a field and throw down with bodyweight

Take it outdoors!

exercises, put on inline skates, surf, ski, paddleboard, or even just go for a walk downtown.

Some of the activities I lead and advocate at my own gym are hill running, stair sprints, and running on a variety of terrains, such as sand, dirt, grass, and trails. Many general physical skills, such as accuracy, coordination, agility, and balance, are best developed during outdoor activity, on a less forgiving surface than an even and consistent rubber gym floor. Running a trail involves hundreds of microcorrections of the knee, ankle, and foot, and requires a heightened sense of sight and awareness of your surroundings. And while this quality of precision of movement can certainly be applied in the gym, it cannot be learned in the gym.

Some of my favorite exercises and workouts can easily be performed outdoors. For example, an assortment of push/pull and open/close movements can be done at a playground, using bars, steps, and benches. All of this is good stuff, activating different motor patterns in your body and muscles you might not even have known you have.

Changing things up in your routine is a potent recipe for promoting performance gains. It's not just a matter of changing the workout; it's exploring and experiencing all the variables. Different levels of heat, elevation, surface, and time of day are a few of the ways to add variety and keep body and mind in a state of development. And without a doubt, the spiritual impact of exercise in the sun, on the surface of the earth, is profound.

You are limited only by your imagination when it comes to getting outside of the box. Here are some of my favorites to get you started.

MY FAVORITE OUTDOOR WORKOUTS

GREAT BODYWEIGHT "FITNESS OUTSIDE THE BOX" WORKOUTS

The principles of the *Victory* program provide a framework for you to develop you own programming, adding your unique perspective, imagination, and intuition into your programming. Although the workouts below are some of my favorites, I encourage you to take what works and make changes where you feel they are necessary. I've also included some of my personal records on the workouts—in the event you're up for a challenge, try to best them!

BURGENER GONE MAD

- 150 burpees for time

Named after the great Olympic lifting coach, Mike Burgener. This can be done anywhere—your local park would work just fine. My goal for this challenging workout is to bring it home in 10:00 or less.

SUPER SUN

- Four rounds for time:

- 50 squats,

- Run 400 meters,

- 30 hand-release push-ups

Following the first round, note your "split time" (the time it took you to complete one round). Try to keep your remaining three rounds within 30 seconds of that first round. Doing this workout at the beach is priceless. I've also varied this session by subbing an ocean swim for the run. I swim straight out into the ocean, and each time my right hand strokes through the water is "one rep." After I complete 40 reps, I turn around and swim back to shore.

GOT LEGS?

- Four rounds for time:

- Run 400 meters,

- 50 squats

This was one of Coach Glassman's favorite outdoor workouts, and we conducted it on a variety of outdoor surfaces, from sand to grass. An extra challenge is to perform this workout on a hill, running up and down, and performing the squats at the bottom.

EMOM, ADD A 10-METER SPRINT

- Minute one: sprint 10 meters

- Minute two: sprint 20 meters, etc.

Sand presents a challenging surface for this workout. It's best on a 10-meter course, because ideally you are changing directions at the end of each sprint. I advocate touching one hand to the surface just beyond the cone or 10-meter line you've established. I performed this workout with UFC legend Gray Maynard and Six-time world champion boxer Robert "The Ghost" Guerrero at Pleasure Point Beach in Santa Cruz, California, on a regular basis. The goal is to work up to 7 rounds. Then, for a real challenge, when you can no longer maintain the interval, rest one full minute, then start over at your last successful interval, working back down to a 1x10-meter sprint.

TABATA MASHUP

A Tabata squat session consists of 8 rounds of 20 seconds of squats followed by 10 seconds rest, followed by as many push-ups or pull-ups as possible in 4 minutes. Your score is the lowest round of Tabata squats, multiplied by the total number of push-ups or pull-ups completed. Choosing the lowest round of Tabata squats forces you to remain consistent during each round.

RAW STRENGTH

- 10-9-8 (down to 1) repetitions of:

- Alternating single-leg squats (pistols)

- Alternating single-arm push-ups

- Rest 2:00 then:

- 2:00 of squats (using both legs)

- 2:00 of push-ups (using both arms)

This is a great workout that starts out developing terrific strength and ends by developing endurance and stamina.

Those are some ideas for vigorous training options, each of which can be scaled to your current level of fitness. If you want to make it even simpler, just put on your running shoes and get out on the trails for an hour, hop on the mountain bike and explore—or finally learn a new sport you have always wanted to try. All of these will do wonders to energize and invigorate your training.

PLAY SPORTS

Have you ever wanted to learn to surf? Or do a marathon or an ultramarathon? Or join a soccer league? Do you think your exercise program gets in the way? Quite the opposite—the *Victory* plan is an optimal first step toward making your sports dream come true.

There are plenty of workout programs out there that promise to get you from the couch to the starting line of a marathon or triathlon. But here's the problem—without a general fitness foundation and a strengthened set of general skills, along with a knowledge of how to move well, you are going to struggle with the training. Also, when it comes to an activity with a lot of repetitive movements, not knowing how to move well can have adverse effects on your joints and body.

The *Victory* workout plans address several general athletic skills: cardiovascular/respiratory endurance, stamina, strength, flexibility, power, speed, coordination, agility, balance, and accuracy. Together, these build in you a super-sound athletic foundation and will allow you to pick up a new sport more readily and enjoy it with less risk of acute or chronic injuries.

Furthermore, the converse is true: Taking on a new sport will do wonders for your fitness goals. It will energize your training with a new goal, and it will draw greater nuances from the general skills into your body and mind as what you learn will be fed back into your growing capacities.

I learned this the hard way.

In 2009, I hit a major snag during the qualification for the CrossFit Games. I had been training consistently for eight years, and had continued to improve every year. I had put my training to use in various roles, including serving in the Army and as a SWAT operator with the sheriff's office in Santa Cruz. I considered myself well prepared for the unknown and the unknowable. I had even been dubbed the "Original Firebreather." Given all this, qualifying for the Games was surely in my wheelhouse.

But there's always a reality check in the pursuit of preparing for the unknown and unknowable. It's always ready to put you to the test and weed out weaknesses in your training program. It will keep you humble.

As it did with me in 2009.

Despite having plenty of strength, power, stamina, and an assortment of skills in the gym, I had my Achilles' heel: double unders. I didn't like doing them and, because I let that get in the way of my judgment, I hadn't practiced them and mastered them. This was a costly mistake, and it bit me in 2009 when a workout to qualify for the games was comprised of deadlifts (no problem!) and double unders, a jump-rope movement where the rope passes beneath your feet two times per swing. The double-under nature of this movement ramps up the cardiovascular demand and taxes a range of skills.

I'll jump to the painful conclusion here: Despite an all-out effort, I couldn't do the double unders well enough to qualify. I fell short. As one of the early leaders of the CrossFit movement, this was embarrassing.

I could draw a line from my inability to perform this movement directly to an ego conflict. Ego often leads us to choose workouts that we like and are good at, and urges us to avoid movements that we don't feel confident with.

My failure at what had become a routine skill in CrossFit offered me a potent and valuable lesson.

When I did not qualify for the Games that year, I went back to the drawing board and worked hard to improve my double unders. In a matter of weeks I had become adept at them. All it took was intention and consistent attention, and an obsession to learn a skill.

But here the story took an unexpected and powerful turn. Because I had addressed a deficiency in my set of basic skills—in this case, my coordination and accuracy, honed by the double unders—the adaptations the training incurred spread throughout my athletic capacity. Indeed, my entire athletic foundation took a leap forward, and skills outside of the purely athletic realm also got a bounce.

For example, I noted that my skills on the shooting range jumped up a level. I had been in law enforcement for nearly a decade, and all of a sudden, I was a better shooter and had better weapon-manipulation skills because my accuracy and coordination skills with the double under had improved. I learned that improving capacity in skills requiring coordination, accuracy, agility, and balance do not exist in a vacuum, and instead spread throughout the entire body and mind, and lend improvement to any other skill requiring capacity within these same domains.

Improving my double unders also improved my speed and skill with plyometric box jumps. I could jump down from a box and fire right back up with a much quicker reaction force.

In other words, moving the lever up on one skill can send waves throughout the systems in such a way that it's expressed in gym movements, as well as movements outside of the gym.

And when it comes to sports, there's a real payoff. Because, after you have spent time working on those general athletic skills through the kind of training outlined in this book, you have a great advantage in learning a new sport. Those general skills are hardwired into each and every sport in unique ways, and you will find that you pick up other sports swiftly.

This is one of the keys to longevity: keeping things interesting. Again, this is part of the appeal of functional-fitness conditioning. You can put it to use in having fun with different sports.

The icing on the cake is this: By learning new sports, you send new dimensions of skill through the entire system. Nuances that come with a new sport will help you make the next PR in the gym. It might even help your double unders!

One of my training partners years ago was an amazing athlete and the only person I've ever met who can do a strict one-arm pull-up with both arms. How did he get that rare skill? It came from mountain climbing!

Team sports, individual sports, outdoor activities, indoor activities—everything and anything from track to month-long sea-kayaking trips. Find a sport that intrigues you and jump in!

PUTTING IT ALL TOGETHER

TERMINOLOGY:

AMRAP = as many rounds (or repetitions) as possible

Threshold = your 100% maximum effort

Box Breathing = 4-count breathing exercise

Mantra or Affirmation = your personal belief statement

EMOM = every minute on the minute

RM = repetition max effort in weightlifting

First Words = the warrior practice of mindful speaking

MLPRP = meal preparation

LEVEL ONE

The 21-day *Victory* level one training plan is designed to build your confidence, develop technique and increase capacity in a combined weightlifting and gymnastic conditioning program. In addition, this plan will set the foundation for establishing the concepts of an integrated and holistic program as you begin to experience the benefits of daily breathwork, meditation, and the spiritual disciples of memorizing and repeating God's Word.

In the words of my dear friend and longtime
mentor, Mark Divine, the founder of SEALFIT,
Unbeatable Mind and Kokoro Yoga ....
"Stay the course! You've got this!"

LEVEL ONE

DAY ONE

❏ *First words*
❏ *5 minutes of meditation*
❏ *4 rounds of box breathing*
❏ *Eyes Closed: 10 repetitions of Bible verse*

BASELINE WORKOUT

AMRAP in 10:00 of:
   Squat, 30 repetitions
   Push-up, 20 repetitions
   Pull-up, 10 repetitions
   (use a band if necessary, or ring row)

From 10:00 to 15:00:
   Find your 1 repetition power clean

MEAL PLAN

BREAKFAST:
P: _____
C: _____
F: _____

LUNCH:
P: _____
C: _____
F: _____

DINNER:
P: _____
C: _____
F: _____

SNACK:
P: _____
C: _____
F: _____

DAY TWO

❏ *First words*
❏ *5 minutes of meditation*
❏ *4 rounds of box breathing*
❏ *Eyes Closed: 10 repetitions of Bible verse*

AMRAP MASH-UP TEST #1

AMRAP 1:00 of jump rope
Rest 1:00

AMRAP 1:00 of kettlebell swing (35 lb. / 25 lb.)
Rest 2:00 and determine your 30% threshold

EMOM for 10:00 (5 rounds of each):
   Odd minutes = 30% threshold for jump rope
   Even minutes = 30% threshold for kettlebell
   swing

MEAL PLAN

BREAKFAST:
P: _____
C: _____
F: _____

LUNCH:
P: _____
C: _____
F: _____

DINNER:
P: _____
C: _____
F: _____

SNACK:
P: _____
C: _____
F: _____

LEVEL ONE

DAY THREE

- ❏ *First words*
- ❏ *5 minutes of meditation*
- ❏ *4 rounds of box breathing*
- ❏ *Eyes Closed: 10 repetitions of Bible verse*

Thruster, 5,3,1,1,1 repetitions
(work up to a 1RM) then:
Rest 2:00 and find your 30% threshold of 1RM

AMRAP in 12:00 of:
Run 400 meters (or row 400 meters)
10 ring rows
5 thrusters (30% 1RM)

MEAL PLAN

BREAKFAST:
P: _____
C: _____
F: _____

LUNCH:
P: _____
C: _____
F: _____

DINNER:
P: _____
C: _____
F: _____

SNACK:
P: _____
C: _____
F: _____

DAY FOUR

- ❏ *First words*
- ❏ *5 minutes of meditation*
- ❏ *4 rounds of box breathing*
- ❏ *Eyes Closed: 10 repetitions of Bible verse*

Fitness Outside the Box
(walk, run, hike, swim, surf, play!)

Meal Preparation – Based on your Zone allotment of food, prepare three Zone friendly meals for the next three days of training, for a total of 9 meals. This is your minimum! You can prepare (pre-cook, measure, weigh, store in Tupperware, etc.) additional meals if you would like. Remember that proper nutrition (both the nutrition of your body AND your mind!) is absolutely vital to your overall health and fitness.

MEAL PLAN

BREAKFAST:
P: _____
C: _____
F: _____

LUNCH:
P: _____
C: _____
F: _____

DINNER:
P: _____
C: _____
F: _____

SNACK:
P: _____
C: _____
F: _____

LEVEL ONE

DAY FIVE

- ❏ *First words*
- ❏ *5 minutes of meditation*
- ❏ *4 rounds of box breathing*
- ❏ *Eyes Closed: 10 repetitions of Bible verse*

AMRAP MASH-UP TEST #2

AMRAP in 1:00 of wall ball
   (20 lb. / 14 lb. – 10 ft. / 8ft.)
Rest 1:00

AMRAP in 1:00 of pull-up
   (use a band if necessary)
Rest 2:00 and determine your 30% threshold

EMOM for 12:00 (6 rounds of each)
   Odd minutes = 30% threshold for wall ball
   Even minutes = 30% threshold for pull-up

MEAL PLAN

BREAKFAST:
P: _____
C: _____
F: _____

LUNCH:
P: _____
C: _____
F: _____

DINNER:
P: _____
C: _____
F: _____

SNACK:
P: _____
C: _____
F: _____

DAY SIX

- ❏ *First words*
- ❏ *5 minutes of meditation*
- ❏ *4 rounds of box breathing*
- ❏ *Eyes Closed: 10 repetitions of Bible verse*

AMRAP MASH-UP TEST #3

AMRAP in 1:00 of knee to elbow
Rest 1:00

AMRAP in 1:00 of box jump (20 in. / 16 in.)
Rest 1:00

AMRAP 1:00 of push-up
Rest 2:00 and determine your 40% threshold

Every 3 minutes for 15:00 (5 rounds each)
   Minute 1 = 40% threshold for knee to elbow
   Minute 2 = 40% threshold for box jump
   Minute 3 = 40% threshold for push-up

MEAL PLAN

BREAKFAST:
P: _____
C: _____
F: _____

LUNCH:
P: _____
C: _____
F: _____

DINNER:
P: _____
C: _____
F: _____

SNACK:
P: _____
C: _____
F: _____

— LEVEL ONE —

DAY SEVEN

- ❏ *First words*
- ❏ *5 minutes of meditation*
- ❏ *4 rounds of box breathing*
- ❏ *Eyes Closed: 10 repetitions of Bible verse*

Bench press, 5,3,1,1,1 repetitions
(work up to 1RM bench press)

Back squat, 5,3,1,1,1 repetitions
(work up to a 1RM squat)

Rest 2:00 and determine 30% of 1RM bench and 1RM squat then:

Four rounds for time:
Run 400 meters (or row 400 meters)
Back squat, 9 repetitions (30% 1RM)
Bench press, 6 repetitions (30% 1RM)

MEAL PLAN

BREAKFAST:

P: _____

C: _____

F: _____

LUNCH:

P: _____

C: _____

F: _____

DINNER:

P: _____

C: _____

F: _____

SNACK:

P: _____

C: _____

F: _____

DAY EIGHT

- ❏ *First words*
- ❏ *5 minutes of meditation*
- ❏ *4 rounds of box breathing*
- ❏ *Eyes Closed: 10 repetitions of Bible verse*

Fitness Outside the Box
(walk, run, hike, swim, surf, play!)

Meal Preparation – Based on your Zone allotment of food, prepare three Zone friendly meals for the next three days of training, for a total of 9 meals. This is your minimum! You can prepare (pre-cook, measure, weigh, store in Tupperware, etc.) additional meals if you would like. Remember that proper nutrition (both the nutrition of your body AND your mind!) is absolutely vital to your overall health and fitness.

MEAL PLAN

BREAKFAST:

P: _____

C: _____

F: _____

LUNCH:

P: _____

C: _____

F: _____

DINNER:

P: _____

C: _____

F: _____

SNACK:

P: _____

C: _____

F: _____

LEVEL ONE

DAY NINE

- ❏ *First words*
- ❏ *5 minutes of meditation*
- ❏ *4 rounds of box breathing*
- ❏ *Eyes Closed: 10 repetitions of Bible verse*

AMRAP MASH-UP EVOLUTION #1 (FORMERLY TEST #1)

EMOM for 12:00 (6 rounds of each):

Odd minutes = 40% threshold for jump rope

Even minutes = 40% threshold for kettlebell swing

MEAL PLAN

BREAKFAST:
P: _____
C: _____
F: _____

LUNCH:
P: _____
C: _____
F: _____

DINNER:
P: _____
C: _____
F: _____

SNACK:
P: _____
C: _____
F: _____

DAY TEN

- ❏ *First words*
- ❏ *5 minutes of meditation*
- ❏ *4 rounds of box breathing*
- ❏ *Eyes Closed: 10 repetitions of Bible verse*

On a 10:00 running clock:

Power clean, 30 repetitions (30% 1RM)

10 burpees

Power clean, 30 repetitions (30% 1RM)

Note: For this workout, your "score" is your final set of power cleans.

MEAL PLAN

BREAKFAST:
P: _____
C: _____
F: _____

LUNCH:
P: _____
C: _____
F: _____

DINNER:
P: _____
C: _____
F: _____

SNACK:
P: _____
C: _____
F: _____

LEVEL ONE

DAY ELEVEN

- ❏ *First words*
- ❏ *5 minutes of meditation*
- ❏ *4 rounds of box breathing*
- ❏ *Eyes Closed: 10 repetitions of Bible verse*

AMRAP MASH-UP EVOLUTION #2 (FORMERLY TEST #2)

EMOM for 10:00 (5 rounds of each)
  Odd minutes = 40% threshold for wall ball
  Even minutes = 40% threshold for pull-up

MEAL PLAN

BREAKFAST:
P: _____
C: _____
F: _____

LUNCH:
P: _____
C: _____
F: _____

DINNER:
P: _____
C: _____
F: _____

SNACK:
P: _____
C: _____
F: _____

DAY TWELVE

- ❏ *First words*
- ❏ *5 minutes of meditation*
- ❏ *4 rounds of box breathing*
- ❏ *Eyes Closed: 10 repetitions of Bible verse*

Fitness Outside the Box
  (walk, run, hike, swim, surf, play!)

Meal Preparation – Based on your Zone allotment of food, prepare three Zone friendly meals for the next three days of training, for a total of 9 meals. This is your minimum! You can prepare (pre-cook, measure, weigh, store in Tupperware, etc.) additional meals if you would like. Remember that proper nutrition (both the nutrition of your body AND your mind!) is absolutely vital to your overall health and fitness.

MEAL PLAN

BREAKFAST:
P: _____
C: _____
F: _____

LUNCH:
P: _____
C: _____
F: _____

DINNER:
P: _____
C: _____
F: _____

SNACK:
P: _____
C: _____
F: _____

LEVEL ONE

DAY THIRTEEN

❏ *First words*

❏ *5 minutes of meditation*

❏ *4 rounds of box breathing*

❏ *Eyes Closed: 10 repetitions of Bible verse*

AMRAP MASH-UP EVOLUTION #3 (FORMERLY TEST #3)

Every 3 minutes for 12:00 (4 rounds each)

 Minute 1 = 40% threshold for knee to elbow

 Minute 2 = 40% threshold for box jump

 (20 in. / 16 in.)

 Minute 3 = 40% threshold for push-up

 (Repeat for 15:00)

MEAL PLAN

BREAKFAST:

P: _____

C: _____

F: _____

LUNCH:

P: _____

C: _____

F: _____

DINNER:

P: _____

C: _____

F: _____

SNACK:

P: _____

C: _____

F: _____

DAY FOURTEEN

❏ *First words*

❏ *5 minutes of meditation*

❏ *4 rounds of box breathing*

❏ *Eyes Closed: 10 repetitions of Bible verse*

Shoulder press, 5,3,1,1,1 repetitions (establish a 1RM)

Rest 2:00 and determine 30% of your 1RM press then:

Four rounds for time:

 Push-press, 15 repetitions (30% 1RM)

 30 squats

 Pull-up, 10 repetitions (or sub Ring Row)

Note: Although the 1RM that you will establish is your press, in the workout, utilize the push-press.

MEAL PLAN

BREAKFAST:

P: _____

C: _____

F: _____

LUNCH:

P: _____

C: _____

F: _____

DINNER:

P: _____

C: _____

F: _____

SNACK:

P: _____

C: _____

F: _____

LEVEL ONE

DAY FIFTEEN

- ❏ *First words*
- ❏ *5 minutes of meditation*
- ❏ *4 rounds of box breathing*
- ❏ *Eyes Closed: 10 repetitions of Bible verse*

AMRAP MASH-UP EVOLUTION #1 (FORMERLY TEST #1)

EMOM for 10:00 (5 rounds of each)

Odd minutes = 40% threshold for jump rope

Even minutes = 40% threshold for kettlebell swing (35 lb. / 25 lb.)

MEAL PLAN

BREAKFAST:

P: _____

C: _____

F: _____

LUNCH:

P: _____

C: _____

F: _____

DINNER:

P: _____

C: _____

F: _____

SNACK:

P: _____

C: _____

F: _____

DAY SIXTEEN

- ❏ *First words*
- ❏ *5 minutes of meditation*
- ❏ *4 rounds of box breathing*
- ❏ *Eyes Closed: 10 repetitions of Bible verse*

Fitness Outside the Box
(walk, run, hike, swim, surf, play!)

Meal Preparation – Based on your Zone allotment of food, prepare three Zone friendly meals for the next three days of training, for a total of 9 meals. This is your minimum! You can prepare (pre-cook, measure, weigh, store in Tupperware, etc.) additional meals if you would like. Remember that proper nutrition (both the nutrition of your body AND your mind!) is absolutely vital to your overall health and fitness.

MEAL PLAN

BREAKFAST:

P: _____

C: _____

F: _____

LUNCH:

P: _____

C: _____

F: _____

DINNER:

P: _____

C: _____

F: _____

SNACK:

P: _____

C: _____

F: _____

LEVEL ONE

DAY SEVENTEEN

- ❏ *First words*
- ❏ *5 minutes of meditation*
- ❏ *4 rounds of box breathing*
- ❏ *Eyes Closed: 10 repetitions of Bible verse*

AMRAP in 15:00 of:
- Run 400 meters (or row 400 meters)
- 10 burpees
- 5 thrusters (30% 1RM)

MEAL PLAN

BREAKFAST:
P: _____
C: _____
F: _____

LUNCH:
P: _____
C: _____
F: _____

DINNER:
P: _____
C: _____
F: _____

SNACK:
P: _____
C: _____
F: _____

DAY EIGHTEEN

- ❏ *First words*
- ❏ *5 minutes of meditation*
- ❏ *4 rounds of box breathing*
- ❏ *Eyes Closed: 10 repetitions of Bible verse*

Three rounds for time:
- Jump rope, 100 repetitions
- Kettlebell swing, 20 repetitions (35 lb. / 25 lb.)
- Ring row, 10 repetitions

MEAL PLAN

BREAKFAST:
P: _____
C: _____
F: _____

LUNCH:
P: _____
C: _____
F: _____

DINNER:
P: _____
C: _____
F: _____

SNACK:
P: _____
C: _____
F: _____

LEVEL ONE

DAY NINETEEN

❏ *First words*

❏ *5 minutes of meditation*

❏ *4 rounds of box breathing*

❏ *Eyes Closed: 10 repetitions of Bible verse*

Complete as many reps as possible in 10 minutes following the rep scheme below:

Power clean, 3 repetitions (30% 1RM)
3 knee to elbow
Power clean, 6 repetitions
6 knee to elbow
Power clean, 9 repetitions
9 knee to elbow
Power clean, 12 repetitions
12 knee to elbow
Power clean, 5 repetitions
15 knee to elbow

This is a timed workout. If you complete the round of 15, go on to 18. If you complete 18, go on to 21, etc.

MEAL PLAN

BREAKFAST:

P: _____

C: _____

F: _____

LUNCH:

P: _____

C: _____

F: _____

DINNER:

P: _____

C: _____

F: _____

SNACK:

P: _____

C: _____

F: _____

DAY TWENTY

❏ *First words*

❏ *5 minutes of meditation*

❏ *4 rounds of box breathing*

❏ *Eyes Closed: 10 repetitions of Bible verse*

Fitness Outside the Box
(walk, run, hike, swim, surf, play!)

Meal Preparation – Based on your Zone allotment of food, prepare three Zone friendly meals for the next three days of training, for a total of 9 meals. This is your minimum! You can prepare (pre-cook, measure, weigh, store in Tupperware, etc.) additional meals if you would like. Remember that proper nutrition (both the nutrition of your body AND your mind!) is absolutely vital to your overall health and fitness.

MEAL PLAN

BREAKFAST:

P: _____

C: _____

F: _____

LUNCH:

P: _____

C: _____

F: _____

DINNER:

P: _____

C: _____

F: _____

SNACK:

P: _____

C: _____

F: _____

LEVEL ONE

DAY TWENTY-ONE

❏ *First words*

❏ *5 minutes of meditation*

❏ *4 rounds of box breathing*

❏ *Eyes Closed: 10 repetitions of Bible verse*

BASELINE WORKOUT RETEST

AMRAP in 10:00 of:

Squat, 30 repetitions

Push-up, 20 repetitions

Pull-up, 10 repetitions

(use a band if necessary)

From 10:00 to 15:00

Find your 1 repetition power clean

MEAL PLAN

BREAKFAST:

P: _____

C: _____

F: _____

LUNCH:

P: _____

C: _____

F: _____

DINNER:

P: _____

C: _____

F: _____

SNACK:

P: _____

C: _____

F: _____

Congratulations! You've just created an amazing amount of momentum in your life, and begun the process of integrating your mind, body, and spirit. It's time to increase the challenge, which means you'll also be increasing the rewards. Here we go!

LEVEL TWO

The 21-day *Victory* intermediate training plan takes your integrated fitness to the next level. In the next 21 days, you'll begin to increase the intensity of your workouts, and the duration of your mind and spirit practices. In my experience and in the feedback of thousands of athletes I've coached, the real benefit of the integrated training will be noticed "between the ears". To provide you with some inspiration, let me share the words of Coach Glassman that dramatically shaped my life:

> *"The greatest adaptation to CrossFit*
> *(or any physical training program)*
> *takes place between the ears."*

—Coach Greg Glassman, Founder of CrossFit

LEVEL TWO

DAY ONE

- ❏ *First words*
- ❏ *10 minutes of meditation*
- ❏ *4 rounds of box breathing*
- ❏ *Eyes Closed: 15 repetitions of Bible verse*

BASELINE WORKOUT

AMRAP in 10:00 of:
  Squat, 50 repetitions
  Push-up, 30 repetitions
  Pull-up, 10 repetitions

From 10:00 to 15:00
  Find your 1 repetition power clean

MEAL PLAN

BREAKFAST:
P: _____
C: _____
F: _____

LUNCH:
P: _____
C: _____
F: _____

DINNER:
P: _____
C: _____
F: _____

SNACK:
P: _____
C: _____
F: _____

DAY TWO

- ❏ *First words*
- ❏ *10 minutes of meditation*
- ❏ *4 rounds of box breathing*
- ❏ *Eyes Closed: 15 repetitions of Bible verse*

AMRAP MASH-UP TEST #1

AMRAP in 1:00 of jump rope (double under)
Rest 1:00

AMRAP in 1:00 of kettlebell swing (35 lb. / 25 lb.)
Rest 2:00 and determine your 40% threshold

EMOM for 12:00 (6 rounds of each)
  Odd minutes = 40% threshold for jump rope
  (double under)
  Even minutes = 40% threshold for kettlebell
  swing

MEAL PLAN

BREAKFAST:
P: _____
C: _____
F: _____

LUNCH:
P: _____
C: _____
F: _____

DINNER:
P: _____
C: _____
F: _____

SNACK:
P: _____
C: _____
F: _____

LEVEL TWO

DAY THREE

❏ *First words*

❏ *10 minutes of meditation*

❏ *4 rounds of box breathing*

❏ *Eyes Closed: 15 repetitions of Bible verse*

Thruster, 5,3,1,1,1 repetitions
  (work up to a 1RM weight) then:
Rest 2:00 and find your 50% threshold of 1RM

AMRAP in 12:00 of:
  Run 400 meters (or row 400 meters)
  10 burpees
  5 thrusters (50% 1RM)

MEAL PLAN

BREAKFAST:

P: _____

C: _____

F: _____

LUNCH:

P: _____

C: _____

F: _____

DINNER:

P: _____

C: _____

F: _____

SNACK:

P: _____

C: _____

F: _____

DAY FOUR

❏ *First words*

❏ *10 minutes of meditation*

❏ *4 rounds of box breathing*

❏ *Eyes Closed: 15 repetitions of Bible verse*

Fitness Outside the Box
  (walk, run, hike, swim, surf, play!)

Meal Preparation – Based on your Zone allotment of food, prepare three Zone friendly meals for the next three days of training, for a total of 9 meals. This is your minimum! You can prepare (pre-cook, measure, weigh, store in Tupperware, etc.) additional meals if you would like. Remember that proper nutrition (both the nutrition of your body AND your mind!) is absolutely vital to your overall health and fitness.

MEAL PLAN

BREAKFAST:

P: _____

C: _____

F: _____

LUNCH:

P: _____

C: _____

F: _____

DINNER:

P: _____

C: _____

F: _____

SNACK:

P: _____

C: _____

F: _____

LEVEL TWO

DAY FIVE

❏ First words

❏ 10 minutes of meditation

❏ 4 rounds of box breathing

❏ Eyes Closed: 15 repetitions of Bible verse

AMRAP MASH-UP TEST #2

AMRAP in 1:00 of wall ball (20 lb. / 14 lb. – 10 ft.)

Rest 1:00

AMRAP in 1:00 of pull-up

Rest 2:00 and determine your 40% threshold

EMOM for 12:00 (6 rounds of each)
  Odd minutes = 40% threshold for wall ball
  Even minutes = 40% threshold for pull-up

MEAL PLAN

BREAKFAST:
P: _____
C: _____
F: _____

LUNCH:
P: _____
C: _____
F: _____

DINNER:
P: _____
C: _____
F: _____

SNACK:
P: _____
C: _____
F: _____

DAY SIX

❏ First words

❏ 10 minutes of meditation

❏ 4 rounds of box breathing

❏ Eyes Closed: 15 repetitions of Bible verse

AMRAP MASH-UP TEST #3

AMRAP in 1:00 of toes to bar
Rest 1:00
AMRAP in 1:00 of box jumps (24 in. / 20 in.)
Rest 1:00
AMRAP in 1:00 of push-ups
Rest 2:00 and determine your 40% threshold

Every 3 minutes for 15:00 (5 rounds each)
  Minute 1 = 40% threshold for toes to bar
  Minute 2 = 40% threshold for box jumps
  Minute 3 = 40% threshold for push-ups
  (Repeat for 15:00, 5 rounds at each station)

MEAL PLAN

BREAKFAST:
P: _____
C: _____
F: _____

LUNCH:
P: _____
C: _____
F: _____

DINNER:
P: _____
C: _____
F: _____

SNACK:
P: _____
C: _____
F: _____

LEVEL TWO

DAY SEVEN

- ❏ *First words*
- ❏ *10 minutes of meditation*
- ❏ *4 rounds of box breathing*
- ❏ *Eyes Closed: 15 repetitions of Bible verse*

Bench press, 5,3,1,1,1 repetitions
(work up to 1RM bench press)

Back squat, 5,3,1,1,1 repetitions
(work up to a 1RM squat)

Rest 2:00 and determine 50% of 1RM bench and 1RM squat then:

Four rounds for time:
Run 400 meters (or row 400 meters)
Back squat, 12 repetitions (50% 1RM)
Bench press, 9 repetitions (50% 1RM)
10 pull-ups

MEAL PLAN

BREAKFAST:
P: _____
C: _____
F: _____

LUNCH:
P: _____
C: _____
F: _____

DINNER:
P: _____
C: _____
F: _____

SNACK:
P: _____
C: _____
F: _____

DAY EIGHT

- ❏ *First words*
- ❏ *10 minutes of meditation*
- ❏ *4 rounds of box breathing*
- ❏ *Eyes Closed: 15 repetitions of Bible verse*

Fitness Outside the Box
(walk, run, hike, swim, surf, play!)

Meal Preparation – Based on your Zone allotment of food, prepare three Zone friendly meals for the next three days of training, for a total of 9 meals. This is your minimum! You can prepare (pre-cook, measure, weigh, store in Tupperware, etc.) additional meals if you would like. Remember that proper nutrition (both the nutrition of your body AND your mind!) is absolutely vital to your overall health and fitness.

MEAL PLAN

BREAKFAST:
P: _____
C: _____
F: _____

LUNCH:
P: _____
C: _____
F: _____

DINNER:
P: _____
C: _____
F: _____

SNACK:
P: _____
C: _____
F: _____

LEVEL TWO

DAY NINE

❑ *First words*

❑ *10 minutes of meditation*

❑ *4 rounds of box breathing*

❑ *Eyes Closed: 15 repetitions of Bible verse*

AMRAP MASH-UP EVOLUTION #1 (FORMERLY TEST #1)

EMOM for 12:00 (6 rounds of each)
Odd minutes = 50% threshold for jump rope (double under)
Even minutes = 50% threshold for kettlebell swing

MEAL PLAN

BREAKFAST:

P: _____

C: _____

F: _____

LUNCH:

P: _____

C: _____

F: _____

DINNER:

P: _____

C: _____

F: _____

SNACK:

P: _____

C: _____

F: _____

DAY TEN

❑ *First words*

❑ *10 minutes of meditation*

❑ *4 rounds of box breathing*

❑ *Eyes Closed: 15 repetitions of Bible verse*

Clean and jerk, 5,3,1,1,1 repetitions
(work up to a 1RM weight) then:
Rest 2:00 and find your 50% threshold of 1RM

On a 10:00 running clock,
Clean and Jerk, 30 repetitions (50% 1RM)
Burpee & Pull-up, 10 repetitions
Clean and Jerk, AMRAP (50% 1RM)

Note: For this workout, your "score" is your final set of clean and jerks. A "Burpee Pull-up" means a full range of motion Burpee, then as you jump into the air, instead of clapping your hands, grab the Pull-up bar, and complete a Pull-up. Come off the bar, and repeat for the prescribed repetitions.

MEAL PLAN

BREAKFAST:

P: _____

C: _____

F: _____

LUNCH:

P: _____

C: _____

F: _____

DINNER:

P: _____

C: _____

F: _____

SNACK:

P: _____

C: _____

F: _____

LEVEL TWO

DAY ELEVEN

❏ *First words*
❏ *10 minutes of meditation*
❏ *4 rounds of box breathing*
❏ *Eyes Closed: 15 repetitions of Bible verse*

AMRAP MASH-UP EVOLUTION 2 (FORMERLY TEST #2)

EMOM for 12:00 (6 rounds of each)
  Odd minutes = 50% threshold for wall ball
  Even minutes = 50% threshold for pull-up

MEAL PLAN

BREAKFAST:
P: _____
C: _____
F: _____

LUNCH:
P: _____
C: _____
F: _____

DINNER:
P: _____
C: _____
F: _____

SNACK:
P: _____
C: _____
F: _____

DAY TWELVE

❏ *First words*
❏ *10 minutes of meditation*
❏ *4 rounds of box breathing*
❏ *Eyes Closed: 15 repetitions of Bible verse*

Fitness Outside the Box
  (walk, run, hike, swim, surf, play!)

Meal Preparation – Based on your Zone allotment of food, prepare three Zone friendly meals for the next three days of training, for a total of 9 meals. This is your minimum! You can prepare (pre-cook, measure, weigh, store in Tupperware, etc.) additional meals if you would like. Remember that proper nutrition (both the nutrition of your body AND your mind!) is absolutely vital to your overall health and fitness.

MEAL PLAN

BREAKFAST:
P: _____
C: _____
F: _____

LUNCH:
P: _____
C: _____
F: _____

DINNER:
P: _____
C: _____
F: _____

SNACK:
P: _____
C: _____
F: _____

LEVEL TWO

DAY THIRTEEN

❏ First words

❏ 10 minutes of meditation

❏ 4 rounds of box breathing

❏ Eyes Closed: 15 repetitions of Bible verse

AMRAP MASH-UP EVOLUTION #3 (FORMERLY TEST #3)

Every 3 minutes for 15:00 (5 rounds each)

    Minute 1 = 50% threshold for toes to bar

    Minute 2 = 50% threshold for box jump

    (24 in. / 20 in.)

    Minute 3 = 50% threshold for push-up

    (Repeat for 15:00)

MEAL PLAN

BREAKFAST:

P: _____

C: _____

F: _____

LUNCH:

P: _____

C: _____

F: _____

DINNER:

P: _____

C: _____

F: _____

SNACK:

P: _____

C: _____

F: _____

DAY FOURTEEN

❏ First words

❏ 10 minutes of meditation

❏ 4 rounds of box breathing

❏ Eyes Closed: 15 repetitions of Bible verse

Shoulder press, 5,3,1,1,1 repetitions
    (establish a 1RM)

Rest 2:00 and determine 50% of your 1RM press then:

Four rounds for time:

    Run 400 meters (or row 400 meters)

    Push-press, 15 repetitions (50% 1RM)

    20 weighted alternating lunges, 10 each leg

    (25 lb. / 15 lb.)

Note: Although the 1RM that you will establish is your press, in the workout, utilize the push-press.

MEAL PLAN

BREAKFAST:

P: _____

C: _____

F: _____

LUNCH:

P: _____

C: _____

F: _____

DINNER:

P: _____

C: _____

F: _____

SNACK:

P: _____

C: _____

F: _____

LEVEL TWO

DAY FIFTEEN

❏ *First words*
❏ *10 minutes of meditation*
❏ *4 rounds of box breathing*
❏ *Eyes Closed: 15 repetitions of Bible verse*

AMRAP MASH-UP EVOLUTION #1 (FORMERLY TEST #1)

EMOM for 10:00 (5 rounds of each)
Odd minutes = 60% threshold for double under
Even minutes = 60% threshold for kettlebell swing (35 lb. / 25 lb.)

MEAL PLAN

BREAKFAST:
P: _____
C: _____
F: _____

LUNCH:
P: _____
C: _____
F: _____

DINNER:
P: _____
C: _____
F: _____

SNACK:
P: _____
C: _____
F: _____

DAY SIXTEEN

❏ *First words*
❏ *10 minutes of meditation*
❏ *4 rounds of box breathing*
❏ *Eyes Closed: 15 repetitions of Bible verse*

Fitness Outside the Box
   (walk, run, hike, swim, surf, play!)

Meal Preparation – Based on your Zone allotment of food, prepare three Zone friendly meals for the next three days of training, for a total of 9 meals. This is your minimum! You can prepare (pre-cook, measure, weigh, store in Tupperware, etc.) additional meals if you would like. Remember that proper nutrition (both the nutrition of your body AND your mind!) is absolutely vital to your overall health and fitness.

MEAL PLAN

BREAKFAST:
P: _____
C: _____
F: _____

LUNCH:
P: _____
C: _____
F: _____

DINNER:
P: _____
C: _____
F: _____

SNACK:
P: _____
C: _____
F: _____

LEVEL TWO

DAY SEVENTEEN

- ❏ *First words*
- ❏ *10 minutes of meditation*
- ❏ *4 rounds of box breathing*
- ❏ *Eyes Closed: 15 repetitions of Bible verse*

AMRAP in 20:00 of:
  Run 400 meters (or row 400 meters)
  10 burpees
  5 thrusters (60% 1RM)

MEAL PLAN

BREAKFAST:
P: _____
C: _____
F: _____

LUNCH:
P: _____
C: _____
F: _____

DINNER:
P: _____
C: _____
F: _____

SNACK:
P: _____
C: _____
F: _____

DAY EIGHTEEN

- ❏ *First words*
- ❏ *10 minutes of meditation*
- ❏ *4 rounds of box breathing*
- ❏ *Eyes Closed: 15 repetitions of Bible verse*

Deadlift 5,3,1,1,1 repetitions (establish a 1RM)
Rest 4:00 and determine 40% 1RM deadlift then:

For time:
  Deadlift, 21 repetitions (40% 1RM)
  21 bar dips
  15 deadlifts
  15 bar dips
  9 deadlifts
  9 bar dips

MEAL PLAN

BREAKFAST:
P: _____
C: _____
F: _____

LUNCH:
P: _____
C: _____
F: _____

DINNER:
P: _____
C: _____
F: _____

SNACK:
P: _____
C: _____
F: _____

LEVEL TWO

DAY NINETEEN

❏ *First words*
❏ *10 minutes of meditation*
❏ *4 rounds of box breathing*
❏ *Eyes Closed: 15 repetitions of Bible verse*

AMRAP EVOLUTION #3

Every 3 minutes for 15:00 (5 rounds each):
    Minute 1 = 60% threshold for toes to bar
    Minute 2 = 60% threshold for box jump
    (24 in. / 20 in.)
    Minute 3 = 60% threshold for push-up
    (Repeat for 15:00)

MEAL PLAN

BREAKFAST:
P: _____
C: _____
F: _____

LUNCH:
P: _____
C: _____
F: _____

DINNER:
P: _____
C: _____
F: _____

SNACK:
P: _____
C: _____
F: _____

DAY TWENTY

❏ *First words*
❏ *10 minutes of meditation*
❏ *4 rounds of box breathing*
❏ *Eyes Closed: 15 repetitions of Bible verse*

Fitness Outside the Box
    (walk, run, hike, swim, surf, play!)

Meal Preparation – Based on your Zone allotment of food, prepare three Zone friendly meals for the next three days of training, for a total of 9 meals. This is your minimum! You can prepare (pre-cook, measure, weigh, store in Tupperware, etc.) additional meals if you would like. Remember that proper nutrition (both the nutrition of your body AND your mind!) is absolutely vital to your overall health and fitness.

MEAL PLAN

BREAKFAST:
P: _____
C: _____
F: _____

LUNCH:
P: _____
C: _____
F: _____

DINNER:
P: _____
C: _____
F: _____

SNACK:
P: _____
C: _____
F: _____

LEVEL TWO

DAY TWENTY-ONE

❏ *First words*

❏ *10 minutes of meditation*

❏ *4 rounds of box breathing*

❏ *Eyes Closed: 15 repetitions of Bible verse*

BASELINE WORKOUT RETEST

AMRAP in 10:00 of:

   Squat, 50 repetitions

   Push-up, 30 repetitions

   Pull-up, 10 repetitions

From 10:00 to 15:00

   Find your 1 repetition power clean)

MEAL PLAN

BREAKFAST:

P: _____

C: _____

F: _____

LUNCH:

P: _____

C: _____

F: _____

DINNER:

P: _____

C: _____

F: _____

SNACK:

P: _____

C: _____

F: _____

Congratulations! You are now over half-way through the 9-week *Victory* training plan. Stay positive and focused, and "feed the courage wolf!" because the next 21 day cycle will be the most challenging yet.

— LEVEL THREE —

I am so proud of you! If you're embarking on the 21-day *Victory* advanced training plan, that means you've achieved what many people initially considered impossible. I know firsthand how challenging the physical workouts can be. Furthermore, just like everyone else, there are days when I question the benefit of an integrated practice. These are the days I have to "double down" on my positive self-talk and really focus on "feeding the wolf of courage!" I've discovered that when I overcome my own self-doubt, I can then easily overcome other challenges the world brings to my door. Oftentimes when I am in the presence of my mentors, they remind and encourage me to realize that the worlds most successful, happy, fulfilled, and influential people always "win first in their mind" and then on the field of battle. Therefore, use the next 21 days to instill in yourself a commitment to achieve your unlimited potential. You've got this!

"BUIYATAOO = Believe Unconditionally In Yourself And The Ability Of Others."

—Greg Amundson

LEVEL THREE

DAY ONE

- ❏ *First words*
- ❏ *20 minutes of meditation*
- ❏ *8 rounds of box breathing and 10 rounds of Nadi Shodhana*
- ❏ *Eyes Closed: 20 repetitions of Bible verse*

BASELINE WORKOUT

AMRAP in 10:00 of:

Squat, 20 repetitions

Toes to bar, 10 repetitions

Push-up, 20 repetitions

Pull-up, 10 repetitions

From 10:00 to 15:00

Find your 1 repetition clean and jerk

MEAL PLAN

BREAKFAST:

P: _____

C: _____

F: _____

LUNCH:

P: _____

C: _____

F: _____

DINNER:

P: _____

C: _____

F: _____

SNACK:

P: _____

C: _____

F: _____

DAY TWO

- ❏ *First words*
- ❏ *20 minutes of meditation*
- ❏ *8 rounds of box breathing and 10 rounds of Nadi Shodhana*
- ❏ *Eyes Closed: 20 repetitions of Bible verse*

AMRAP MASH-UP TEST #1

AMRAP in 1:00 of double under

Rest 1:00

AMRAP in 1:00 of kettlebell swing (53 lb. / 35 lb.)

Rest 2:00 and determine your 40% threshold

EMOM for 14:00 (7 rounds of each)

Odd minutes = 40% threshold for double under

Even minutes = 40% threshold for kettlebell swing

MEAL PLAN

BREAKFAST:

P: _____

C: _____

F: _____

LUNCH:

P: _____

C: _____

F: _____

DINNER:

P: _____

C: _____

F: _____

SNACK:

P: _____

C: _____

F: _____

—— LEVEL THREE ——

DAY THREE

- ❏ First words
- ❏ 20 minutes of meditation
- ❏ 8 rounds of box breathing and 10 rounds of Nadi Shodhana
- ❏ Eyes Closed: 20 repetitions of Bible verse

Thruster, 5,3,1,1,1 repetitions
   (work up to a 1RM weight) then:
Rest 2:00 and find your 60% threshold of 1RM

AMRAP in 12:00 of:
   Run 400 meters (or row 400 meters)
   10 burpees over barbell (lateral jumps over barbell)
   5 thrusters (60% 1RM)

MEAL PLAN

BREAKFAST:
P: _____
C: _____
F: _____

LUNCH:
P: _____
C: _____
F: _____

DINNER:
P: _____
C: _____
F: _____

SNACK:
P: _____
C: _____
F: _____

DAY FOUR

- ❏ First words
- ❏ 20 minutes of meditation
- ❏ 8 rounds of box breathing and 10 rounds of Nadi Shodhana
- ❏ Eyes Closed: 20 repetitions of Bible verse

Fitness Outside the Box
   (walk, run, hike, swim, surf, play!)

Meal Preparation – Based on your Zone allotment of food, prepare three Zone friendly meals for the next three days of training, for a total of 9 meals. This is your minimum! You can prepare (pre-cook, measure, weigh, store in Tupperware, etc.) additional meals if you would like. Remember that proper nutrition (both the nutrition of your body AND your mind!) is absolutely vital to your overall health and fitness.

MEAL PLAN

BREAKFAST:
P: _____
C: _____
F: _____

LUNCH:
P: _____
C: _____
F: _____

DINNER:
P: _____
C: _____
F: _____

SNACK:
P: _____
C: _____
F: _____

LEVEL THREE

DAY FIVE

- ❏ *First words*
- ❏ *20 minutes of meditation*
- ❏ *8 rounds of box breathing and 10 rounds of Nadi Shodhana*
- ❏ *Eyes Closed: 20 repetitions of Bible verse*

AMRAP MASH-UP TEST #2

AMRAP in 1:00 of wall ball (20 lb. / 14 lb. – 10 ft.)
Rest 1:00

AMRAP in 1:00 of pull-up
Rest 2:00 and determine your 40% threshold

EMOM for 12:00 (6 rounds of each)
   Odd minutes = 40% threshold for wall ball
   Even minutes = 40% threshold for pull-up

MEAL PLAN

BREAKFAST:
P: _____
C: _____
F: _____

LUNCH:
P: _____
C: _____
F: _____

DINNER:
P: _____
C: _____
F: _____

SNACK:
P: _____
C: _____
F: _____

DAY SIX

- ❏ *First words*
- ❏ *20 minutes of meditation*
- ❏ *8 rounds of box breathing and 10 rounds of Nadi Shodhana*
- ❏ *Eyes Closed: 20 repetitions of Bible verse*

AMRAP MASH-UP TEST #3

AMRAP in 1:00 of toes to bar
Rest 1:00

AMRAP in 1:00 of box jumps (24 / 20 inch box)
Rest 1:00

AMRAP in 1:00 of Concept2 row (or double under)
Rest 2:00 and determine your 40% threshold

Every 3 minutes for 15:00 (5 rounds each)
   Minute 1 = 40% threshold for toes to bar
   Minute 2 = 40% threshold for box jump
   Minute 3 = 40% threshold for Concept2 row
   (Repeat for 15:00; 5 rounds at each station)

MEAL PLAN

BREAKFAST:
P: _____
C: _____
F: _____

LUNCH:
P: _____
C: _____
F: _____

DINNER:
P: _____
C: _____
F: _____

SNACK:
P: _____
C: _____
F: _____

LEVEL THREE

DAY SEVEN

- ❏ *First words*
- ❏ *20 minutes of meditation*
- ❏ *8 rounds of box breathing and 10 rounds of Nadi Shodhana*
- ❏ *Eyes Closed: 20 repetitions of Bible verse*

Bench press 5,3,1,1,1 repetitions
(work up to 1RM bench press)

Back squat 5,3,1,1,1 repetitions
(work up to a 1RM squat)

Rest 2:00 and determine 50% of 1RM bench and 1RM squat then:

Four rounds for time:
Run 400 meters (or row 400 meters)
Back squat, 15 repetitions (50% 1RM)
Bench press, 12 repetitions (50% 1RM)
Rope climb, 2 trips (or 12 pull-ups)

MEAL PLAN

BREAKFAST:
P: _____
C: _____
F: _____

LUNCH:
P: _____
C: _____
F: _____

DINNER:
P: _____
C: _____
F: _____

SNACK:
P: _____
C: _____
F: _____

DAY EIGHT

- ❏ *First words*
- ❏ *20 minutes of meditation*
- ❏ *8 rounds of box breathing and 10 rounds of Nadi Shodhana*
- ❏ *Eyes Closed: 20 repetitions of Bible verse*

Fitness Outside the Box
(walk, run, hike, swim, surf, play!)

Meal Preparation – Based on your Zone allotment of food, prepare three Zone friendly meals for the next three days of training, for a total of 9 meals. This is your minimum! You can prepare (pre-cook, measure, weigh, store in Tupperware, etc.) additional meals if you would like. Remember that proper nutrition (both the nutrition of your body AND your mind!) is absolutely vital to your overall health and fitness.

MEAL PLAN

BREAKFAST:
P: _____
C: _____
F: _____

LUNCH:
P: _____
C: _____
F: _____

DINNER:
P: _____
C: _____
F: _____

SNACK:
P: _____
C: _____
F: _____

LEVEL THREE

DAY NINE

- ❏ *First words*
- ❏ *20 minutes of meditation*
- ❏ *8 rounds of box breathing and 10 rounds of Nadi Shodhana*
- ❏ *Eyes Closed: 20 repetitions of Bible verse*

AMRAP MASH-UP EVOLUTION #1 (FORMERLY TEST #1)

EMOM for 14:00 (7 rounds of each)
   Odd minutes = 50% threshold for jump rope
   Even minutes = 50% threshold for kettlebell swing

MEAL PLAN

BREAKFAST:
P: _____
C: _____
F: _____

LUNCH:
P: _____
C: _____
F: _____

DINNER:
P: _____
C: _____
F: _____

SNACK:
P: _____
C: _____
F: _____

DAY TEN

- ❏ *First words*
- ❏ *20 minutes of meditation*
- ❏ *8 rounds of box breathing and 10 rounds of Nadi Shodhana*
- ❏ *Eyes Closed: 20 repetitions of Bible verse*

Clean and jerk, 5,3,1,1,1 repetitions
   (work up to a 1RM weight) then:
Rest 2:00 and find your 60% threshold of 1RM

On a 10:00 running clock:
   Clean and jerk, 30 repetitions (60% 1RM)
   GI Jane burpee pull-up, 30 repetitions
   Clean and jerk, AMRAP (60% 1RM)

Note: For this workout, your "score" is your final set of clean and jerks.

MEAL PLAN

BREAKFAST:
P: _____
C: _____
F: _____

LUNCH:
P: _____
C: _____
F: _____

DINNER:
P: _____
C: _____
F: _____

SNACK:
P: _____
C: _____
F: _____

LEVEL THREE

DAY ELEVEN

- ❏ First words
- ❏ 20 minutes of meditation
- ❏ 8 rounds of box breathing and 10 rounds of Nadi Shodhana
- ❏ Eyes Closed: 20 repetitions of Bible verse

AMRAP MASH-UP EVOLUTION 2 (FORMERLY TEST #2)

EMOM for 12:00 (6 rounds of each)
   Odd minutes = 50% threshold for wall ball
   Even minutes = 50% threshold for pull-up

MEAL PLAN

BREAKFAST:
P: _____
C: _____
F: _____

LUNCH:
P: _____
C: _____
F: _____

DINNER:
P: _____
C: _____
F: _____

SNACK:
P: _____
C: _____
F: _____

DAY TWELVE

- ❏ First words
- ❏ 20 minutes of meditation
- ❏ 8 rounds of box breathing and 10 rounds of Nadi Shodhana
- ❏ Eyes Closed: 20 repetitions of Bible verse

Fitness Outside the Box
   (walk, run, hike, swim, surf, play!)

Meal Preparation – Based on your Zone allotment of food, prepare three Zone friendly meals for the next three days of training, for a total of 9 meals. This is your minimum! You can prepare (pre-cook, measure, weigh, store in Tupperware, etc.) additional meals if you would like. Remember that proper nutrition (both the nutrition of your body AND your mind!) is absolutely vital to your overall health and fitness.

MEAL PLAN

BREAKFAST:
P: _____
C: _____
F: _____

LUNCH:
P: _____
C: _____
F: _____

DINNER:
P: _____
C: _____
F: _____

SNACK:
P: _____
C: _____
F: _____

LEVEL THREE

DAY THIRTEEN

❏ First words

❏ 20 minutes of meditation

❏ 8 rounds of box breathing and 10 rounds of Nadi Shodhana

❏ Eyes Closed: 20 repetitions of Bible verse

AMRAP MASH-UP EVOLUTION #3 (FORMERLY TEST #3)

Every 3 minutes for 15:00 (5 rounds each)
Minute 1 = 50% threshold for toes to bar
Minute 2 = 50% threshold for box jump (24 in. / 20 in.)
Minute 3 = 50% threshold for Concept2 row
(Repeat for 15:00)

MEAL PLAN

BREAKFAST:
P: _____
C: _____
F: _____

LUNCH:
P: _____
C: _____
F: _____

DINNER:
P: _____
C: _____
F: _____

SNACK:
P: _____
C: _____
F: _____

DAY FOURTEEN

❏ First words

❏ 20 minutes of meditation

❏ 8 rounds of box breathing and 10 rounds of Nadi Shodhana

❏ Eyes Closed: 20 repetitions of Bible verse

Shoulder press 5,3,1,1,1 repetitions (establish a 1RM)
Rest 2:00 and determine 50% of your 1RM press then:

Four rounds for time:
Run 400 meters (or row 400 meters)
Push-press, 15 repetitions (50% 1RM)
20 pistols (10 each leg)

Note: Although the 1RM that you will establish is your press, in the workout, utilize the push-press.

MEAL PLAN

BREAKFAST:
P: _____
C: _____
F: _____

LUNCH:
P: _____
C: _____
F: _____

DINNER:
P: _____
C: _____
F: _____

SNACK:
P: _____
C: _____
F: _____

LEVEL THREE

DAY FIFTEEN

❏ *First words*

❏ *20 minutes of meditation*

❏ *8 rounds of box breathing and 10 rounds of Nadi Shodhana*

❏ *Eyes Closed: 20 repetitions of Bible verse*

AMRAP MASH-UP EVOLUTION #1 (FORMERLY TEST #1)

EMOM for 12:00 (6 rounds of each)

Odd minutes = 60% threshold for double under

Even minutes = 60% threshold for kettlebell

swing (53 lb. / 35 lb.)

MEAL PLAN

BREAKFAST:

P: _____

C: _____

F: _____

LUNCH:

P: _____

C: _____

F: _____

DINNER:

P: _____

C: _____

F: _____

SNACK:

P: _____

C: _____

F: _____

DAY SIXTEEN

❏ *First words*

❏ *20 minutes of meditation*

❏ *8 rounds of box breathing and 10 rounds of Nadi Shodhana*

❏ *Eyes Closed: 20 repetitions of Bible verse*

Fitness Outside the Box
   (walk, run, hike, swim, surf, play!)

Meal Preparation – Based on your Zone allotment of food, prepare three Zone friendly meals for the next three days of training, for a total of 9 meals. This is your minimum! You can prepare (pre-cook, measure, weigh, store in Tupperware, etc.) additional meals if you would like. Remember that proper nutrition (both the nutrition of your body AND your mind!) is absolutely vital to your overall health and fitness.

MEAL PLAN

BREAKFAST:

P: _____

C: _____

F: _____

LUNCH:

P: _____

C: _____

F: _____

DINNER:

P: _____

C: _____

F: _____

SNACK:

P: _____

C: _____

F: _____

— LEVEL THREE —

DAY SEVENTEEN

- ❏ *First words*
- ❏ *20 minutes of meditation*
- ❏ *8 rounds of box breathing and 10 rounds of Nadi Shodhana*
- ❏ *Eyes Closed: 20 repetitions of Bible verse*

AMRAP in 20:00 of:
    Run 400 meters (or row 400 meters)
    10 burpees over barbell (lateral jumps over barbell)
    5 thrusters (70% 1RM)

MEAL PLAN

BREAKFAST:
P: _____
C: _____
F: _____

LUNCH:
P: _____
C: _____
F: _____

DINNER:
P: _____
C: _____
F: _____

SNACK:
P: _____
C: _____
F: _____

DAY EIGHTEEN

- ❏ *First words*
- ❏ *20 minutes of meditation*
- ❏ *8 rounds of box breathing and 10 rounds of Nadi Shodhana*
- ❏ *Eyes Closed: 20 repetitions of Bible verse*

Deadlift, 5,3,1,1,1 repetitions (establish a 1RM)
Rest 4:00 and determine 50% 1RM deadlift then:

For time:
    Deadlift, 21 repetitions (50% 1RM)
    21 ring dips
    15 deadlifts
    15 ring dips
    9 deadlifts
    9 ring dips

MEAL PLAN

BREAKFAST:
P: _____
C: _____
F: _____

LUNCH:
P: _____
C: _____
F: _____

DINNER:
P: _____
C: _____
F: _____

SNACK:
P: _____
C: _____
F: _____

LEVEL THREE

DAY NINETEEN

- ❏ *First words*
- ❏ *20 minutes of meditation*
- ❏ *8 rounds of box breathing and 10 rounds of Nadi Shodhana*
- ❏ *Eyes Closed: 20 repetitions of Bible verse*

Complete 1 round for time:

Run 800 meters,

Power clean, 50 repetitions (50% of 1RM clean and jerk)

Handstand push-up, 30 repetitions

MEAL PLAN

BREAKFAST:

P: _____

C: _____

F: _____

LUNCH:

P: _____

C: _____

F: _____

DINNER:

P: _____

C: _____

F: _____

SNACK:

P: _____

C: _____

F: _____

DAY TWENTY

- ❏ *First words*
- ❏ *20 minutes of meditation*
- ❏ *8 rounds of box breathing and 10 rounds of Nadi Shodhana*
- ❏ *Eyes Closed: 20 repetitions of Bible verse*

Fitness Outside the Box
  (walk, run, hike, swim, surf, play!)

Meal Preparation – Based on your Zone allotment of food, prepare three Zone friendly meals for the next three days of training, for a total of 9 meals. This is your minimum! You can prepare (pre-cook, measure, weigh, store in Tupperware, etc.) additional meals if you would like. Remember that proper nutrition (both the nutrition of your body AND your mind!) is absolutely vital to your overall health and fitness.

MEAL PLAN

BREAKFAST:

P: _____

C: _____

F: _____

LUNCH:

P: _____

C: _____

F: _____

DINNER:

P: _____

C: _____

F: _____

SNACK:

P: _____

C: _____

F: _____

LEVEL THREE

DAY TWENTY-ONE

❏ First words

❏ 20 minutes of meditation

❏ 8 rounds of box breathing and 10 rounds of
  Nadi Shodhana

❏ Eyes Closed: 20 repetitions of Bible verse

BASELINE WORKOUT RETEST

AMRAP in 10:00 of:

  Squat, 20 repetitions

  Toes to bar, 10 repetitions (or knees to elbow)

  Push-up, 20 repetitions

  Pull-up, 10 repetitions (scale as appropriate)

From 10:00 to 15:00

  Find your 1 repetition clean and jerk

MEAL PLAN

BREAKFAST:

P: _____

C: _____

F: _____

LUNCH:

P: _____

C: _____

F: _____

DINNER:

P: _____

C: _____

F: _____

SNACK:

P: _____

C: _____

F: _____

Congratulations! You've done it. Outstanding work! You have created an amazing amount of momentum in your life, and begun the process of integrating your mind, body, and spirit. I encourage you to continue to exercise, meditate and box breathe on a daily basis.

INDEX

(1) Dan Brule' has been an instrumental mentor and guide in my study of pranayama and breath-mastery. His book *Just Breathe* (Atria/Enliven Books, 2018) is a masterpiece and I resource that I highly recommend.

(2) Deepak Chopra. *The Seven Spiritual Laws of Success.* Amber-Allen Publishing, San Rafael, CA. 1994.

(3) Sun Tzu. *The Art of War.* Everyman's Library Classic Series, New York, NY. 2018.

(4) Greg Amundson. *Above All Else.* Eagle Rise Publishing, Virginia Beach, VA. 2018.

(5) Greg Amundson. *Firebreather Fitness.* Velo Press, Boulder, CO. 2018.

(6) Mark Divine, Navy SEAL Commander (Ret). Founder of SEALFIT and author of New York Times bestselling book, *Unbeatable Mind* and *Way of the SEAL.*

(7) Yoga Sutra of Patanjali 2:29

(8) Hebrews 6:19

(9) Job 33:4

(10) Dan Brule'

(11) The Bhagavad Gita 6:13

(12) The four-count breathing exercise is referred to as "Box Breathing" or "Warrior Breath."

(13) The *Ten Mental Attributes of Elite Leadership* were first published in the CrossFit Journal Article Forging Elite Fitness by Greg Amundson, CrossFit Journal, 2012.

(14) My use of brackets within the Scripture for explanation and exegetical purposes.

(15) Brian Hedges. *Christ Formed in You.* Shepherd Press, Colorado Springs, CO. 2010.

(16) Hedges, p. 193.

(17) Hedges, p. 197.

(18) My use of brackets within the Scripture for explanation and exegetical purposes.

(19) Dr. Robert Wiggins, Western Seminary, Professor of Spiritual Disciplines. Portland, Oregon.

(20) The "Jesus Christ Prayer" is also referred to as the "Prayer of the Heart" and is as follows: "Lord Jesus Christ, Son of God, have mercy on me, a sinner." For more information on this prayer, I highly recommend the book *Into The Silent Land* by Martin Laird, Oxford University Press, 2016.

(21) Father Andrew Ceno and I met on the "grinder" at the historic SEALFIT training compound in Encinitas, CA., in early 2012, and became fast friends. He is the Senior Priest of Saint Katherine of Alexandria Orthodox Church in San Diego, and has been an instrumental mentor in my life.

(22) Donald Whitney. *Spiritual Disciplines for the Christian Life.* NavPress, New York, NY. 2016.

(23) D.A. Carson. *Praying With Paul.* Baker Academic, Boulder, CO. 2013.

(24) My use of brackets within the Scripture for explanation and exegetical purposes.

AN ONGOING PROGRAM

Scaled and advanced 21-day cycles. Do you need a 21-day program more within your reach? Or one that's more challenging? Visit my websites GregoryAmundson.com and CrossFitAmundson.com for several additional plans, videos, exercise descriptions and resources. Plus, as a special incentive for your completion of the 21 days plays, all *Victory* program athletes receive a special discount on a private consultation with me. Just use code "21DayFirebreather" upon checkout for any of my mentorship programs available at GregoryAmundson.com/mentor.

Follow Greg online for daily inspiration:

ALSO FROM BESTSELLING AUTHOR GREG AMUNDSON

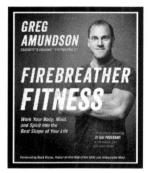

Greg Amundson's effective guides to functional fitness, nutrition, goal-setting, pain tolerance, honing purpose and focus, and exerting control over your mental state are designed to help meet any challenge. Packed with practical advice, vetted training methods, and Amundson's guided workout programs, *Firebreather Fitness* is a must-have resource for athletes, coaches, law enforcement and military professionals, and anyone interested in pursuing the high-performance life. Includes a foreword from *New York Times* bestselling author Mark Divine.

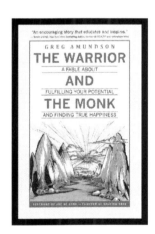

The Warrior and The Monk tells the extraordinary story of a young warrior who seeks the counsel of a wise monk on the universal quest to find true happiness. This is Greg Amundson's #1 Amazon multi-category bestselling book.

ABOUT THE AUTHOR

A graduate of the University of California at Santa Cruz, Greg Amundson has spent nearly twenty years in warrior professions to include assignments as a Special Weapons and Tactics Team Operator (SWAT) and Sniper in Santa Cruz County, a Captain in the United States Army, a Special Agent with the Drug Enforcement Administration (DEA) on the Southwest Border and an Agent on the highly effective Border Enforcement Security Taskforce (BEST) Team.

In addition to his extensive government work, Greg is recognized as a thought leader in the field of integrated wellness practices, and is a prolific author and speaker whose message has positively influenced the lives of thousands of spiritual seekers. A former owner of the nations first CrossFit gym, Greg has traveled around the world teaching functional fitness and self-mastery principles for over nineteen years.

Greg is a Krav Maga Black Belt and honor graduate of the Los Angeles Police Department Handgun Instructor School (HITS). Greg currently serves as a Reserve Peace Officer and Law Enforcement Chaplain in Santa Cruz. Greg is also a graduate student at Western Seminary in San Jose, CA., a four-time #1 Amazon bestselling author, and a founding member of the Eagle Rise Speakers Bureau and Eagle Rise Publishing, which has produced numerous bestselling books.

Connect with Greg at www.GregoryAmundson.com.

KEYNOTES AND SEMINARS

GREG AMUNDSON is one of North America's most electric, encouraging, and motivating professional speakers. Greg has logged more than 10,000 hours of dynamic public speaking on topics including leadership, intrinsic motivation, holistic wellness practices, functional fitness, warrior spirit, and God's Love. Greg speaks around the Country to Law Enforcement Departments on integrating disciplined warrior practices to foster increased Officer Safety while simultaneously generating stronger community relationships.  A plank owner of the highly regarded Eagle Rise Speakers Bureau, Greg is renowned for his ability to transcend boundaries and speak to the heart of Spirituality. His use of captivating storytelling results in a profound and transformational learning experience.

To book Greg Amundson at your next conference or in-house event please visit www.GregoryAmundson.com.

Made in the USA
San Bernardino, CA
09 August 2020